Beyond Kick & Punch

The Complete Fighting Principles Of American Freestyle Karate

Dan Anderson
2002 FSKA World Champion

Beyond Kick & Punch

The Complete Fighting Principles Of American Freestyle Karate

Dan Anderson
2002 FSKA World Champion

Editor: Dan Anderson
Photography: Justin Mangum, Justin Spence
Graphics Consultant: Alexandria Martin
Featuring: Dan Anderson, Pem Wall, Nicole Sindelar

© 2005 Dan Anderson
All Rights Reserved
Compiled in the United States of America

First Release March 2005

Warning

This book is presented only as a means of preserving a unique aspect of the heritage of karate. The author does not make any representation, warranty or guarantee that the techniques described or illustrated in this book will be safe or effective in any self-defense situation or otherwise. You may be injured if you apply or train the techniques illustrated in this book. To minimize the risk of training injury, nothing described or illustrated in this book should be undertaken without personal, expert instruction. In addition, it is essential that you consult a physician regarding whether or not to attempt anything described in this book. Specific self-defense responses illustrated in this book may not be justified in any particular situation in view if all the circumstances or under the applicable federal, state or local law.

Contacting Dan Anderson

Website: http://www.danandersonkarate.com
Postal Mail: P.O. Box 1463 • Gresham, Oregon 97030

Reflections

November 18, 1966. It's my 14th birthday and I am excited. My mother bought me karate lessons for my birthday. I found out from Dave Starkey where he took lessons. Marshal Recreation Center in Vancouver, Washington. Class time was 7:00 PM. I showed up and found out Dave's class time was 7:00. The beginner's class was at 6:00. The instructor, Loren Christensen, must've taken pity on this kid so he sent a blue belt, Tony Leonetti, over to start me on my basics. Straight punch, front kick, downward block, climbing form (zenkutsu dachi - forward stance). Wow! This was excitement. I ripped out the seat of my pants that night but I didn't care. This was karate training! I watched the blue belts spar. How could they go that fast and not kill each other? I was amazed. Much later I found out they were not going fast at all but it sure was amazing to me then. I still remember my classmates. Paul Diment was a body builder. Dave Starkey was a small guy. Fred Wilcox had the boniest shins and brought along his neighbor kid, Jay Eisenlohr. Most of all I remember the instructor, Loren Christensen. He looked like real karate! He was husky, had piercing eyes, and when we trained, he was training with us and harder than the rest of us. Wow!

My second black belt test. I had failed the first one and pestered the chief instructor of our organization to let me retake he test. I was chiefly a kicker back then. He paired me with John Zuber for the sparring portion of the test. John was a short, aggressive, construction worker. I'd hit him with a kick. He'd ignore it and plow right through me with a series of punches, often knocking me through the hanging heavy bags. Over and over again this pattern happened. I failed the test miserably but learned something - don't pester your instructor for a promotion. This test brought to light a major weakness in my sparring - I had no hands.

January, 1970. Another black belt test. This time I was paired with Wayne Lenore. In the sparring we nearly knocked each other out. He caught me with a punch to the head and later I hit him with a knife hand strike to the neck. We went at each other hard. When the black belt board went off to review the test, I overheard Bill Kunkle remark, "That's what brown belts should look like!" "Wild Bill" Kunkle was the best fighter in the school. I thought to myself, "If Bill thinks I'm a good brown belt, that's good enough for me." I didn't even look at the attitude change from my previous black belt test where I'd badgered my teacher to let me test on the basis of a couple tournament victories. The verdict came back - pass. Instead of the partying I had envisioned, I went over to a friends house and quietly relaxed.

Bremerton Washington, summer, 1970. This was my fourth tournament as a black belt. I'm fighting Jerry Williams for the Grand Championship. We are in overtime. I see an opening and decide to shoot a side kick over his shoulder to his head. I take off and nail him for the match. This was my first of over 70 Grand Championships I would win over the years. I found out later that he was thinking the same thing - side kick to the head. I'm glad I moved first.

August, 1972 - The Long Beach International Karate Championships. The "Internationals" was the big daddy of American tournaments at the time. It was a two day affair with over 2,000 competitors. This was my third year fighting in the lightweight black belt division. I was also fighting with a broken right hand. I'd broken it two weeks earlier at a tournament in Vancouver, Washington attempting a board break. The lightweight division was large enough to split it into two separate rings. The winner of each ring would fight each other for first place that night. I won my ring and Byong Yu won the other. Byong Yu was very well known for his flying kicks and being willing to go nose to nose with Joe Lewis, the most feared tournament fighter of his time. Me, I was known for...well, I wasn't known then. I watched Byong Yu warm up for some of his fans and saw something interesting. I noticed he wasn't that fast. I could match him for speed. My confidence rose at that point. In the match for the title, we both ended playing it very cautiously, either willing to commit. The overtime went 19 minutes! The match ended by him hitting me with a body punch. This was the beginning of my national career.

1973 US Karate Championships, Dallas, Texas. Steve Armstrong, father of Isshin-ryu karate in the Northwest, loaned me plane fare to go to the US Championships. I had heard about the ruggedness of Texas fighting but I found out about it in my first match. I was fighting Dennis Passeretti from the New England area. In our first exchange I caught him with the low round kick to the groin and he hit me in the mouth. I thought, "Okay. Either I've got the point for the kick or the point for the contact call." "Kid Pass" got the point for the punch. Our next exchange I hit him low again and this time he drew blood. "Ahhh. This time I have the point for the kick or a point for contact drawing blood." Point to Passeretti for the punch! Whoa! Wake up call. It's 7 seconds into the match and one more point for Passeretti sends me home. I hit him with the next three points: side kick, spinning back kick, side kick for the match. I ended up fighting Demetrius Havanas, the "Golden Greek," for the lightweight title. I did something only a few people ever accomplished - I won a match with the Greek in Texas.

1978 MARS (Martial Arts Ratings System) Karate Championships, Cleveland, Ohio. My good friend Robert Edwards and I went to Cleveland to represent the Pacific Northwest. The funny thing is that in all the years I knew him, we had never fought each other. He went on to win the heavyweight division in decisive fashion. He leg swept every opponent at least once. One opponent he swept out three times in a row. I won the lightweight division. When he and I faced each other for the championship, I told him not to sweep me. Why he ever listened to me I don't know. I'm just glad he did. I ended up winning this match and became the US Martial Arts Ratings System champ.

Against Larry Kelly at the 1979 Mid-America Diamond Nationals

The next year I went to the 1979 Mid-America Diamond Nationals in Minneapolis, Minnesota. This event had the cream of the crop of US karate fighters: Keith Vitali, Ray McCallum, Larry Kelly, Mike Genova, Herb Johnson, John Longstreet, and myself - all top-ten rated fighters. I faced #1 rated Keith Vitali for the lightweight division title. I decided to match whatever he did. If he backed up, I backed up. If he attacked, I attacked. We had one heck of a match and went into overtime. I changed tactics and when he attacked, I backed up just far enough to make him miss and hit him with a counter punch. I later beat Larry Kelly for the Grand Championship. I was #1 in the country...until the next tournament.

I had been in retirement for a good five years or so when the 1990 Goodwill Games were held in Seattle. The AAU held a karate tournament in conjunction with the Goodwill Games. My then-wife Lynn and good friend Fred King were imploring me to compete. I kept telling them, *"Absolutely not! I'm retired! I won't go. I'm done."* I did, however, work out with them as they were competing. One Sunday Fred came up to me and said, *"Danny, I just talked to Karen. Charles Lakes didn't make the team."* I didn't like this at all. You see, an organization I belong to, the Hubbard Dianetics Foundation was one of the sponsors of the Goodwill Games. Charles Lakes was the captain of the 1988 Olympic US gymnastics team and the main "face" for the Hubbard Dianetics Foundation. With him not making the qualifying cut, I knew someone else had to represent the Foundation. I knew it was going to be me. I only had one month to train by this time so I worked on timing and positioning rather than any aerobics. I remember going into the final match in the open weight division. It was hot in the gym and I was dog tired. I watched the match that would determine my opponent for the finals. I spotted that the winner of that match was making one mistake over and over again. He would step first and hit second. This I could take advantage of...and did. Every time he stepped, I came forward and hit him. I ended up winning the gold medal for the open weight division and captained the US "B" Team, which beat the World Champion team from Europe for another gold medal.

2002 Funakoshi Shotokan Karate Association World Championships, Las Vegas, Nevada. Tom Levak told me about this tournament. He'd been trying to get me to go to this or that tournament only to be met with the same answer, "Tom! I'm retired! I'm not interested! No!" Well, this time he had something different to tell me. This was a world championship meet with age divisions that break every five years. It had a 50-54 year old age bracket. This caught my attention. It was also in Las Vegas. Close enough for an inexpensive plane flight and an age division that agreed with me. The one thing I had never won was a world championship so I began training. Everything was going along fine until about two weeks before the event. My sciatic nerve was acting up. Ouch. There went my kicks. No problem.

Wow, all sorts of memories and these only scratch the surface. I've had a great career which culminates in this book. Good reading to you!

Loren Christensen, my first instructor in April 1967. This photo was taken at the Marshal Recreation Center (left photo).
At the 1969 Western States Karate Championships with my second instructor, Mike Engeln. This was my first win as a brown belt (middle photo).
1973 United States Karate Championships lightweight division 1st place trophy. Dallas, Texas (right photo).

Facing off against Pat Bailey to gain a berth on the Pacific Northwest for the 1st WUKO world championships in 1972. I made it on the northwest team but didn't make the cut for the US team (left photo) Posing with the two gold medals I won at the 1990 Seattle Goodwill Games (middle photo). Tom Levak and I with our gold medals from the 4th Funakoshi Shotokan Karate Association World Championships at Las Vegas in 2002 (right photo).

Acknowledgments

This is a tough one because every person I've met in the karate field; whether they have been for me, against me, or neutral has had an impact on my martial arts career. I am a firm believer in never regretting what I have done or has happened. Many times I could have made a better decision and done the right thing but I wouldn't be who I am today or have accomplished all that I have if I changed my life around. So, as odd as it sounds, I acknowledge everyone who had been in my karate life and has influenced it. For better or worse, you have all touched me.

For the purpose of this book there are several people who I'd like to specifically point out and thank.

Pem Wall - Pem is my photo partner for most of the book and he has had a profound impact on my life as an individual being. Back in 1985, I was ready to go to press with my second karate book. The photos had been taken and Unique Publications was ready to go to press with it. There was some rumor floating around that my photo partner was getting into some unethical practices. I was perfectly willing to turn a blind eye to the whole matter as nothing had been put in writing about it nor had he been formally accused. Then Pem sat down with me and very simply and softly said, *"Just do this. Take a look at what he's doing, actually doing, and then make a decision for yourself."* When I did that and confronted what my photo partner was into, I called Unique Publications and told them that we had to retake the photos. I couldn't back my photo partner by having him in the book. The book ended up being dropped. I self published it a number of years later. Pem helped me take and ethical look at the situation. This has influenced me over the years.

Steve Armstrong - Steve is the father of Isshin-ryu karate in the Pacific Northwest. Believe it or not, Steve was the one who had the most faith in my potential in the early years of my competition. He wasn't my instructor - he lived 135 miles away from me but he always treated me as well as any of his students. It was because of him that I took my first step towards becoming a national champion.

Fred King - I've known Fred for 30 years. He has a great background. Fred King was #1 rated tournament fighter in 1980 by Karate Illustrated magazine (KI) for the Northwest; was rated by KI yearbook as the best puncher, and was a Top 20 fighter in US. He's taught for over 30 years in the US and Europe and is only person to receive a dual presentation of Professorship from Professor's Wally Jay and Remy Presas. He has earned black belts in Modern Arnis, Wun Hop Kuen Do, Kajukenbo, American Teachers Association of the Martial Arts, American Karate Association and developed Mo Duk Pai Kung Fu in 1984. He and I have trained together countless times and fought each other in tournaments many times and each has been a barn stormer. He is right there with Pem as far as being a very ethical man and is a huge influence on me in that area.

Grand Master Remy Presas - Although Prof. Presas was not primarily a karate man, he nevertheless, was a huge influence on my way of thinking in the martial arts.

Bill Rookledge & Thomas F. Levak - My first black belts and loyalty in very trying times.

My Gresham, Oregon karate students, past and present - To every one who has trained at my school in the last twenty years. My instructing you has enriched my life and martial arts knowledge.

Loren Christensen - My first karate teacher. I don't think there could be anyone better to start off my karate training than him.

James Reed Anderson & Betty Jean Skiles - My father and mother who supported a 14 year old kids dream.

Marie, Jenelle, Robert, Nicole, Jessica, Alexandria, & Amanda - My wife and family (from oldest to youngest). Wonderful, incredibly beautiful people. Thank you for being with me.

Foreword

I'm so glad that Dan Anderson has been spending the last few years putting down his approach to the fighting arts on paper, specifically in books. A lot of people can claim to have *practiced* the martial arts for many years, even many decades, but few can claim legitimately to have *studied* for many years or decades. There is a difference.

Dan's writing reveals his years of dedicated study of karate and the Filipino stick fighting arts. It shows what he has learned from reading and training with many other martial art greats, champions, masters, professors and gurus. And his writing reveals his sponge-like ability to absorb what he has learned from other veteran fighters and to put that knowledge into action with his particular slant on it.

Beyond Kick & Punch is destined to be a best-seller and to be around for years to come. This is because it's not based on the newest martial arts fad, but rather solid fighting principles and techniques that have served Dan and his legion of students – personal students and his many readers - for years in the tournament ring.

Dan and I began our karate training in the mid 1960's at the Oregon Karate Association. While his journey in the fighting arts took him into the tournament ring where he triumphed to become one of competition's all-time greats, my journey, because of my time in a war zone and 25 years as a cop in a major city, has focused on techniques, concepts and principles for street survival. Well, there is much in *Beyond Kick & Punch* for the analytical street oriented fighter, too. This is because fighting principles are fighting principles, whether the battle is with fists, sticks, knives, guns or missiles.

Don't hesitate to get this book. Unlike other ones on your shelf, you will underline, dog-ear, cover with Post-its, and reference *Beyond Kick & Punch* for years to come.

Loren W. Christensen – 7th dan
www.lwcbooks.com

Foreword

Nearly every month I go down to different book stores, used and new, to see what's new in the martial arts section. Sometimes I buy, most not. I've been doing this for over 35 years. I consider myself a reader and doer in the martial arts arena. I've missed a few months, but rarely, as I've made it up by going weekly sometimes, all in the quest of who's writing what on what. And is it any good? Is it worth reading? And then is it any good after reading it, that it will be in my library?

Many of the books are either "been there, done that", or "badly written", or so simple (and I don't mean fundamentally simple as the law of gravity is fundamentally simple) that you wonder if they are writing to those who are actually literate or not, or have any sense of martial art training or understanding. It's a world of word-garbage sometimes. And then sometimes there's some books that show themselves and stand right out. When you see one that stands up and says — "I'm here, read me" you grab it and read it. And it's a pleasure.
The pleasure is built around any characteristic we deem important: uniqueness, ease of reading, practicality, in depth analysis, etc. What a find. What joy!

I've studied for over 40 years the Martial Arts. I've been banged and bruised. I've gone on the national tournament circuit and did fairly well, I've helped open up Europe to full contact fighting and did a little banging around myself. All in all, I've been living a life of training as much and whenever I can. I mix the physical with the academic whenever I can. The two must meet or we don't progress. The progression comes in the verbal passing of information from teacher to student and from teacher to "the masses" i.e. when someone writes or videos it competent information.. It's a wonderful thing!

Dan Anderson is someone who has done well against the best, continues to study the art, and without a doubt has few peers in the sport karate arena. Dan Anderson had a flair in the ring to be a no-nonsense, let's win kind of guy. He proved it year after year, tournament after tournament. That's just on the physical end. And I can say, without a doubt, after reviewing his book and having spoken with him by the hour, here's someone who not only has something to say but has put it down on paper. And it's worth reading. It's a KEEPER!

What's of interest to the reader is Dan Anderson's ability to define himself by actually analyzing and describing how he did it. This is no fool. This is someone who knows what he's talking about and can back it up, and has! What he used, uses and does is in depth. This is not a "technique" book. As he says in his book, you can get that from your instructor. Really, how many ways can you show a front kick? Different terms maybe, and a few little nuances, but other than that a front kick is a front kick. But ahh, to understand the when, how, where, strategy of delivering a technique or predicting one, now that is knowledge. His other tournament books were well worth reading. This one stands out on it's own and is something that any student, teacher and Master can keep, read and use.
Best,
Fred King

Foreword

Dan Anderson was one of sport karate's finest champions and instructors. He was one of the most intelligent technicians on the tournament circuit. His books on American Freestyle Karate have been a very great teaching aid in learning how to spar properly and to be a consistent winner in competition. Dan will take you through a step-by-step learning process that will help you develop the proper skills and abilities needed to win in the ring. In the book Dan will demonstrate and explain many of the techniques and strategies that made him a Champion and will make you one also.

Steve Fisher
(Steve Fisher is one of the premier champions of American point fighting competition. He and I came up together as budding young champions in the Golden Age of American tournaments, the 1970's. Steve is a protege of national champion Mike Stone and Shorin-ryu karate master Tadashi Yamashita. He is a five-time Top Ten rated champion in his own right and has trained a number of champions as well. Steve currently operates a karate school in Culver City, California.)

Steve Fisher (L) battling Robert Harris. Photos by Mary Townsley.

Foreword

I find myself in a rather unique position in that I have known Dan Anderson for more years than I usually like to admit to. Even more unique, is I have been fortunate enough to see him as a young gentleman on the tournament circuit in the heyday of the creation of Sport Karate, as a fierce competitor, and champion. Something few are left to testify about, and after running the International Karate Championships for twelve years, I have seen them all.

I watched Dan ply his trade in a completely unique fashion successfully, and then have the foresight to create his own perspective in writing and publish his groundbreaking book on "American Freestyle Karate."

Not a large person or physically overwhelming by any means, but somehow always in a position to overpowered those who supposedly had more weight, and skill. He dominated the ring like no other, and I knew all along the reason he was so successful. He simply was one of the brightest, smartest guys around.

This coupled with his unique abilities and skills and an unquenchable desire to "win" made him virtually unstoppable. Even on a "bad day" in the ring plagued with nagging injuries or fatigue, he would simply "outsmart" you and get the win.

I have also been witness to something that is completely unique in the world of those who were champions at sport competition. I have watched him grow and mature into a special man. I have seen him explore the martial arts from a completely new perspective as his hairline has receded, and I have watched him grow as a family man and a father.

I feel this latest project is as much a product of his growth as a human being and his interaction with his family, as much as anything he has done in the arts. He has matured into a well-rounded and knowledgeable martial artist and person. This book will prove that to you, and I've been witness to it all. A evolution that, in its entirety, has produced a very special human being and a true "Master" and whatever he chooses to do. That makes me, very lucky.

Ron Chapél, Ph.D.
Sub Level Four Kenpo Concepts

(Dr. Ron Chapél, who was a close personal and family friend of Ed Parker from 1963 until his passing in 1990, studied with Parker privately and continuously during that period. He has been teaching kenpo since 1964 and has been a law enforcement officer for 30 years.

Dr. Ron Chapel from the US is the foremost authority on Sub Level Four Kenpo Concepts. Since the passing of Senior Grandmaster Ed Parker, Dr. Ron Chapel has become a sought after, internationally renowned instructor. He began working on Advanced American Kenpo Concepts with his teacher as part of a book and video series. Dr. Ron Chapel, through Mr. Parker's teachings and his volume of personal notes, continues to develop the Legacy of Grandmaster Parker. Sub Level Four Concepts explore the side of Kenpo that few have seen. Sub Level Four curriculum includes Control Manipulation Theory and Cavity Presses (Nerve Strikes) with Destructive Sequencing. These are the elements of American Kenpo that were explored with him by Senior Grand Master E.K. Parker throughout their almost thirty year relationship. Additionally newer concepts have been developed including Misalignment Technology and use of Spatial Distortion.)

Table Of Contents

1. Introduction — 1
2. Monitoring — 6
3. Timing — 23
4. Distancing — 29
5. Balance — 43
6. Positioning — 55
7. Mobility — 65
8. Knowledge Of Offensive & Defensive Approaches — 79
9. Mechanics — 102
10. Afterword — 103

Appendix - The Value Of Kata Training In The 21st Century — 104

Introduction

Fighting is as old as man. Ever since there have been two people differing on something, there has been fighting. Originally, one could suppose, fighting was only a life and death affair. Man, however, in his constant search for amusement and activity, made a game or sport out of fighting. Weapons such as the sword, spear, and club as well as boxing and various forms of wrestling came into being and "fight as play" became popular. Over the years there has been a difference between fight for real and fight for play. One thing that has remained constant, though, has been the continuing development and refining of techniques of fighting.

Fast forward to the 20th century, the early 1950's in Japan. The students at the various universities there were experimenting with free fighting, *jyu kumite (meeting hands)*. Shotokan karate, at that time, consisted of basics drills called *kihon* and solo exercises called *kata*. The students wanted something more exciting. The following is a quote from Randall Hassell's book "Shotokan Karate – Its' History & Evolution" (www.TamashiiPress.com).

Master Masatoshi Nakayama: *"My seniors...knew only kata; it was the only thing Master Funakoshi taught them. But in my generation, things began to change. The people in my generation were required to study martial arts beginning in grammar school, and continuing all the way through graduation from high school. Karate was not taught in the schools at the time, so all of us had studied judo or kendo. But judo and kendo were centered around combat – throwing an opponent or actually striking an opponent with a sword. So, the idea of combat was deeply ingrained in us, and we really needed the combative aspect that karate lacked. Master Funakoshi understood this, and he began to change his teaching methods to meet the needs of our younger generation. We needed more than just kata all the time, and he realized that things would have to change if he was going to attract young people and see his art grow.*

So, he picked techniques from the kata and began teaching gohon kumite (five-step sparring) based on individual kata techniques. We would step in five times with the same attack while the defender blocked. Then the defender would counter attack. But we had high spirits and if the defender did not counter attack immediately, we would attack him again, and he would be forced to improvise a defense and try to counter again. These actions became the basis for free-sparring. By 1950, virtually all the major styles of karate in Japan were practicing some form of free-sparring."

This new form of training was often nothing more than a bloody pounding of each other but this was the beginning of modern day "free fighting" or sparring. Shown below is an example of *ippon kumite* (1 step sparring) and *sambon kumite* (3 step sparring) is presented on the next page.

sambon kumite

Karate tournament free fighting competition started in the United States around, roughly, 1963. At that time, the best fighters were the ones who had the best techniques and could either dish out or take the most punishment. A noted example of this was when Mike Stone knocked out Pat Burleson with a ridge hand strike at the US Championships in 1963. This was shown on the television program Wide World Of Sports. That was the end of televised karate for more than ten years.

In 1965, something happened that changed karate free fighting in the US and began a revolution in the art. Chuck Norris, a Korean Tang Soo Do stylist (chiefly a kicker), was soundly beaten by Tonny Tulleners. Tonny went through his kicks and beat him with punching techniques. At that time, no one crossed karate style lines. If you trained in Japanese karate, you stayed with Japanese karate, no matter what. Being highly competitive, Chuck crossed the line and sought out Japanese karate instructors to learn how to punch. He became unbeatable after that.

In the next 10 years, karate experienced a technical boom like no other. The free fighting skills skyrocketed and with the influence of Chuck Norris, Joe Lewis and Bruce Lee, karate players began cross training like never before. Shortly before his death, Bruce Lee came out with the offensive and defensive approaches he taught in Jeet Kune Do. In 1975, Joe Lewis published what he called the 25 Fighting Principles. Karate in the US at that point began working beyond technical skills and had crossed over into the formulation of principles and conceptual understanding and mental skills as well.

I began training in karate in 1966. I collected every bit of written material on karate I could get my hands on. I studied and studied everyone and everything. I trained hard and ended up being a local, regional, national, and finally, a world champion in free fighting. To do this, I studied and discerned the basic principles that govern free fighting. Now, to me, free fighting is no mystery. To many it is a mystery to be finally solved or frustratingly forever beyond their grasp.

25 years ago I wrote the first comprehensive book on the subject, **American Freestyle Karate: A Guide To Sparring.** This was during the apex of my tournament career. I was looking for a very thorough book on the various approaches to free sparring but there were none. So, I wrote it myself. It became hugely popular and has been a staple in many a martial artist's library since its publication in 1980. To many it has become the bible of sparring. That first book dealt with approaches to sparring. This book deals with understanding of sparring.

I wrote this book to put the understanding of free fighting skills into the hands of everyone. When I say everyone I mean exactly that. My own competitive background spans across a number of different types of competitive arenas including American point competition, Olympic style taekwondo, traditional Japanese competition, and continuous Chinese free fighting. I have won in all these types of competition.

The original text of this manual was a Christmas present for my senior students and some martial arts friends who I had trained with and were dear to me. This was about 15 years ago. Since then, I have finished up five books on Modern Arnis (Filipino martial art) and another one on karate sparring. My two books on karate, **American Freestyle Karate: A Guide To Sparring** and **Fighting Tactics & Strategies** dealt with basics, offensive and defensive approaches, different tactics and so forth for free fighting. As this book has to do with the principles governing free fighting, this is, logically, the next book in the progression.

A point to bring up here before I really get into the "meat and potatoes" of this text is that I tell my students and people who attend my karate seminars that sparring need not be intuitive. I said this to a black belt at a recent seminar and you should've seen the look of amazement on his face. He asked, "You mean it isn't just something that comes with experience? You mean that sparring can be taught?" Absolutely. There are certain fundamental concepts and principles that apply to the learning of sparring and if one has them, their sparring will advance beyond their expectations. So, let's get on with it. Let's define a couple of terms first.

attribute: *"a quality, property, or characteristic of somebody or something"*
principle: *"an important underlying law or assumption required in a system of thought"*

Many fighters look at the attributes and assets of a fighter and work out how to handle those. What I mean by attributes are such things as speed, power, flexibility, degree of intent and so forth. What I mean by assets are values a fighter has which don't change over time. How tall he is or his personal reach would be an asset.

"Wow! This guy is fast."
"Wow! He's really strong."
"Wow! He can kick over my head."
"Geez, this guy is mean."

Attributes can be developed and can change, for the better or worse. Principles are something else.

A principle is an underlying fundamental, that which all else is based on. I believe if you operate by principles, you can overcome another's attributes. You will always find someone who is faster, stronger, more flexible, etc. than you. I have never met anyone who totally has it all. You use your understanding of principles to aid and develop your attributes. I don't knock great attributes, not at all. But if you only fight by attributes without some kind of fundamental reasoning or why behind them, you are restricted by them.

There was a quote in a book translated by Robert W. Smith (*Secrets Of Shaolin Temple Boxing* – Tuttle) that affected me greatly. Roughly paraphrased it said that in a match between two fighters of equal skill, victory will hinge on the ability to change. In other words, the fighter who isn't in a fixed way of operating or "stuck in his own boat" will win. A fighter who operates on principles is able to change easier and faster than one who isn't.

In this manual I go over the principles of American Freestyle Karate. These are the principles I operate by and teach, both in my school and at seminars.

American Freestyle Karate is the name I gave to my own system of Karate. Here is the breakdown of the name.

AMERICAN - I am an American teaching in America. I speak the language and understand the culture. Although the Oriental values are more popularized, the American culture has many of the same values: truth, hard work, respect, honesty, loyalty, honor, and working together with others. These are what we teach to our students, all good American values.

FREESTYLE - This implies an inclusiveness of all the possibilities. Example: If you can only kick, you will be in trouble if a wrestler gets you on the ground. There are limitations in an only one or two-way approach. American Freestyle Karate includes punching, kicking, joint locking, grappling moves as well as long range to close in fighting. In short, any kind of possible fight situation you might find yourself in is covered in our training.

KARATE - This is a term that is generally understood by all Americans that means an unarmed martial art. Also, it is the art that I studied. If I had studied taekwondo or kung fu, it could've ended being up named American Freestyle Kung Fu or taekwondo.

American Freestyle Karate is not a "take the best from each style" approach. It's just one of being prepared. This gives you the basic viewpoint behind the name of the kind of karate that I do. That it is an American style shows that the evolution of Karate has continued.

Another definition of the word principle: *A fundamental truth, law, doctrine or motivating force upon which others are based.* The bottom line fundamental truth I operate off of is that "free fighting/sparring can be understood."

This is a manual on the 8 principles of American Freestyle Karate as I see them. Actually I feel that all martial arts activity falls in the realm of the following principles, regardless of style or country of origin. This is, stripped down and codified, the results of my nearly 40 years research in the martial arts. These are the principles that I operate by. My viewpoint is that if I can do it, anybody can. The trick is to communicate it in such a manner that another person can <u>duplicate</u> it.

These are the most fundamental fundamentals I have been able to come up with for the attainment of skill in my brand of karate. These are conceptual and mechanical principles. My personal philosophy and ways of teaching the methods/concepts that I use aren't included in here as they would be too many to list and aren't part of the conceptual and mechanical make up of American Freestyle Karate.

I will describe the principles in order of importance as each one has its base in the preceding principle. They are, in order:

1. Monitoring
2. Timing
3. Distancing
4. Balance
5. Positioning
6. Mobility
7. Knowledge of the Offensive and Defensive Approaches
8. Mechanics

The first three are in the *perception* band. These are *very* important. The last 5 are in the *mechanical application* band. In my way of thinking, perception is senior to physical mechanics.

This book chiefly concerns the first six. I will briefly go over the seventh one although I do lay out all the different combination techniques and faking moves that I teach my students. For a full treatise on the subject, you can buy either of my commercial books, **American Freestyle Karate: A Guide To Sparring** or **Tactics And Strategies: World Championship Winning Moves**. I will not go into much detail regarding mechanics (chapter 8) as every martial arts school will teach the mechanics of kicking, punching and so on.

These principles have been touched on in my two previous books on karate sparring. This is the first place where they have been compiled, outlined, and gone over at length. The information in this book is 5th Degree Black Belt level in my system. One interesting note as you read on is that you'll find elements of one principle will overlap into other principles as well. They are interlocking in application.

Note: As this is a book on karate, the applications of these principles are done in stand up mode. These principles, however, can be applied to any form of combatics; striking, grappling, or weapons arts. To monitor your opponent's actions is no different whether you have nothing in your hand or have a weapon, whether you are a striker or grappler. The principles apply in all forms of combat.

A typical battle with my friend, Fred King. He was one of my toughest opponents ever.

1. MONITORING

sub-principle: If you are aware of it, you can handle it.

I look at *monitoring* in several different ways. The first is *attack recognition*. Nearly every system of karate, kung fu, or taekwondo uses some way to handle an attack. They all teach blocking but HOW to recognize WHAT is coming so that they can use the "right" or most efficient defense is missing. I have not come across any method of attack spotting taught by any other teacher that really spots what is coming when it comes to effective defense.

I teach two points of monitoring when spotting attacks VISUALLY. For specifically recognizing what attacks are coming I teach *watching the hands*. For purposes of angling out of the way of your opponent I teach watching the shoulders. These two come under the heading of *specific* and *general* monitoring points.

I never watch my opponent's eyes. I either watch his hands (specific monitoring) or watch his shoulders (general monitoring)

Specific Monitoring - Why watch the opponent's hands? Simple. The student must be able to confront, that is to say, to be there comfortably and not flinch in the face of, the opponent. The most dangerous points of the opponent's body are the hardest to confront so these points are the ones I zero in on. As the student trains on confronting his opponent's attacking agents he becomes more and more comfortable with the attack of their opponent until handling the attacks becomes routine.

When you watch the hands it is important that you do so from the *critical distance line*. The fastest, most powerful, yet least telegraphed *long distance* attack your opponent can throw is the *back leg front kick*. If you are far enough away from your opponent so that he can just touch you, you are on the *firing line* or the critical distance line. This is the closest you can stand to your opponent and still be safe. When you are at that distance your opponent has to make a large movement to get to you. This telegraphs his intentions and makes it easier for you to defend yourself.

too close to your opponent   *too far from your opponent*   *right on the critical distance line*

Now when you are at that distance and are watching the hands, tilt your head down so that you can see their thighs in the underside periphery of your vision, thereby being able to detect a kick coming at you. When you look at the type of kick thrown, you can see the difference in how much tell tale motion is occurring with each kick. The least telegraphing motion is the front kick. The others have too much body action associated with them to be fired without being seen easily.

Seeing the thighs in the periphery of your vision

front kick telegraph

round kick telegraph

side kick telegraph

When you are monitoring your opponent's hands, you aren't watching for recognition of what technique is coming. That is too late. What you are looking for is a telegraph of the technique. You are looking for the *beginning* of the technique. You are looking at the first *four inches of movement* which tells you what is coming. This is crucial. If you are looking to recognize what the move ends up being, you will find out be being hit with it. Spotting the telegraphing action of the technique is the key.

How I do it is this: I watch his hands in conjunction with what I call the *Positional Center Line*. If you use both sides of your opponent's body as outer boundaries and mentally draw a line down the middle of those boundaries, you have the Positional Center Line. It will not matter if your opponent is facing forwards, angled, or sideways to you. He will have a Positional Center Line. How his hands move in relation to that line gives you the information you need to read his attacks.

Simply speaking, if his hand crosses the center line he is set up to throw a back fist sort of strike. If his hand moves away from the center line his strike will come at you in a curve. If it just goes at you from its position, it's coming straight at you. This holds the same for kicks as well.

Beyond Kick & Punch - The Complete Fighting Principles Of American Freestyle Karate

Positional center line for a forward facing position, 45 degree angle facing position, and side facing position

  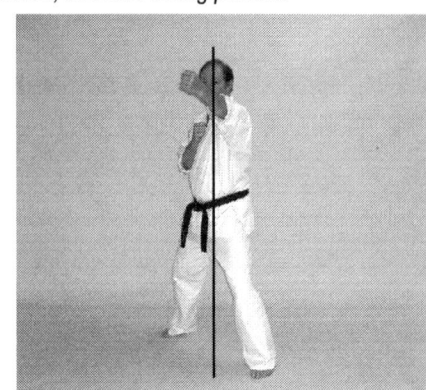

Hand crossing the centerline comes back towards it (back fist style of hitting)

Hand moving away from the positional center line coming back in towards it (hook punch motion)

Front kick and side kick on the positional center line. Round kick and hook kick go away from the positional center line.

When you can monitor your opponent you can use pretty much any method of defense you want. Initially, I teach a two handed blocking system which I call *same siding*. (A side note here: I use the term "blocking" to include all touch forms of defense. I use parrying/deflecting the most. I grew up with the term "blocking" so I continue to use it.) To me, a two handed blocking system leaves you less open for a follow up attack than if you use just one hand to block with. "One armed bandits" are easy to fake out and follow up on. Note: the one place where I do feel a one armed bandit approach is valid is if you counter your opponent's attack right away. If you hesitate, however, you can get hit using the one arm bandit approach.

The above four photos demonstrating the use of same siding.

If you single hand (one armed bandit style) block without an immediate reaction your opponent can follow up on you.

If you are applying what I call a "touch trigger" (the moment your block touches, you counter fire), single hand blocking can be effective.

The reason I teach blocking as the primary defense is that there might be a time when you are backed up in a corner and you can't move away from the attack. Covering up will only result in getting your arms broken, or grabbed and tackled. I've seen this weakness with players who have very good evasive footwork. They've used the footwork as a sly way to not ever confront the attack. Once they get cornered, they cover up, one for one. They don't confront and handle the attack as you have to do with blocking. So, blocking is taught as the primary defense and the beginning of blocking is watching the hands. The most important reason for watching your opponents attacking agents is that it forces a student to confront and handle what they don't want to confront and handle - their opponent.

The above photo sequence is the reason why I teach blocking first. Defensive footwork is great until you get cornered by an aggressive fighter. My partner cuts off every avenue of escape for me until I am caught in the corner. If you can't block when pinned in a corner, you will get beaten.

Monitoring teaches the handling of attacks. The first step of handling attacks is to spot the attack. That means looking at the very things that will attack you and then do something about them. This means blocking the attack and later in my teaching, getting out of the way. But first, you develop your blocking.

General Monitoring - In the way that I teach, after one gets to be a fairly good blocker, then I allow him to angle. In angling you monitor a different part of the body, the shoulders.

The whole idea is that your opponent can't move at all without moving his shoulders so when he moves his shoulders, you angle off of his line of attack. The trick here is to angle - on your recognition of motion, not a recognition of commitment. This is where most people make the mistake. They wait until they are sure that their opponent is coming and then they get hit. Even if you angle and your opponent doesn't come in, you are still off of his line of attack. He will still have to reposition himself in order to set up again. More on this in the section on Mobility.

watching the shoulders

her shoulders moving back

her shoulders moving forward

her shoulders moving to the side

You see from the above photos that I am looking for some sort of tell tale movement of her shoulders. People will do all sorts of minute telegraphing motions with their shoulders. Some rest back on the back leg, pulling the shoulders back. Some will lean forward before they move, making their shoulders come forward slightly. A sideward shift of the shoulders could telegraph a certain kind of kick coming at you. Quite often the movement will be no more than an inch. If you are watching closely and have trained yourself to spot movement, even an inch is enough to forewarn you.

Remember in the introduction when I said that each of the following principles were laid out in order of importance? Well, here is an example of just that. Monitoring is *the* key principle in my book.

When you are going to angle step as a defense, there are three key points you need to know. First, if you are going to move, you must be prepared to move. Quite often one will think his Monitoring is off because he moves out of the way too late. What will be the real reason is that he wasn't prepared to move so his first action was to bend his knees and then move. The bending of the knees is what made him late. The next chapter on Timing goes over this fully. The second key point is to really move off of his line of attack. The analogy I use is one of getting off of the railroad tracks. If you don't fully get off of the tracks, you will get run over. This is the same with angling out of the way of the attack. If you don't get out of the way you will get hit. The third key point is you need room in which to move if you are going to use movement as a defense. If your opponent is too close to you, you will not have time to move out of the way.

Key point #1. I'm not prepared to move - my legs are straight. I see his shoulders drop. Instead of moving, I prepare myself to move by bending my own knees. This is too late because as I am bending my knees, he is already launching his attack.

Key point #1. I'm already prepared to move - my knees are bent. I see his shoulders come forward and I move at the same time. He launches forward but misses me as I am moving out of his way and hitting with a counter strike of my own.

Key point #2. I never step off the line of his attack so, even though I am prepared to move, he hits me anyway.

Beyond Kick & Punch - The Complete Fighting Principles Of American Freestyle Karate

Key point #2. Notice that right when I see his shoulders come forward, I step at an angle, making him miss, and counter strike.

Key point #3. I don't have room to move. I am attempting to move a large body of mass (my body) faster than a small body of mass (his upper body and arm). As he is making a smaller motion (lean and hit), my larger motion (movement of my whole body) is too slow for an effective angle step.

Key point #3. I now have enough distance. Since I step when he telegraphs his motion, I actually step before he steps. This way I can get out of the way of his attack. Note: I go on his telegraph of motion, not on recognizing his commitment of motion. If I step when he steps I might be late and get hit. I step when I see his telegraph prior to his stepping.

After visual monitoring comes *tactile monitoring*. This comes after attainment of 1st Degree Black Belt in my school. This has to do with attack recognition by touch. Here is where you use trapping, joint locking, redirection, sticking, adhering, and so forth. Many Chinese styles emphasize this a lot but don't apply it much in sparring. My feeling is that they have not become comfortable in the presence of their opponent's fast and hard attacks. They haven't learned to confront yet. Here I am not talking about a master of an art. I am talking about your rank and file student and "novice expert," a young black belt.

I've sparred a number of good players whose styles taught sticking hands and so forth and when they demonstrated the art of sticking in either the drills or the self-defense movements, they were pretty good. When we sparred it was a different story. I kept them from applying the sticking skills. The skipped step, I feel, was that they never did get to a point where they could actually handle the tools of the trade (the attacks themselves) comfortably in a non-prearranged manner or in a "hot fight" situation.

Tactile monitoring skill comes after visual monitoring skill. It doesn't come magically all of itself though. You have to train in the sticking hands, pushing hands, adhering, and redirecting drills, flowing locks, and trapping until you get a sensitivity of pressure. Then you can detect what direction your opponent is pushing/pulling and so forth so that you can use it to your best advantage. But this, to me, comes after you can first comfortably confront and handle an attack.

As to handling attacks, I teach my students to block first, then to angle and cover/shield their body, then learn to execute trapping, then joint locking, and finally, neutralizing. These are exact steps. The reason is that it is easier for the student to train confronting an attack that comes at them from far away than one that starts up close. I want to train a person using the proper gradient step so that training doesn't become an overwhelming thing for them. It is easier to confront something farther away than close up, so, that's where you start. You build up to a close-in confront of an attack.

The first of the tactile monitoring drills I teach is called "6 stroke." It is a trapping upon contact drill.

Movement #1 - Beginning from touching the inside of the wrists - Slap and strike

Movement #2 - Fold elbow, grab, & backfist strike

6 Stroke Drill continued

Movement #3 - rear hand threads inside your partner's touch hand, deflects outward, and palm strikes.

Movement #4 - Grab and punch

Movement #5 - Beginning from touching outside of wrists - Drop your hand, grab, and punch.

Movement #6 - Give way to his pressure, trap, and strike.

The next tactile monitoring drill is a simplified version of pushing hands. The key here is to integrate your waist rotation into your "ride and deflect" motion. Beginning from touching the inside of our wrists (1), I push towards my partner. She rolls her body to her left and deflects my push (2,3). At the end of her deflection she returns the push in my direction (4). I rest back on my rear leg, roll to my left side to deflect her push (5). I begin to return push (6) and the cycle begins again.

The next drill is circular sticking. My partner and I move our hands in a circular motion, keeping contact all the time.

My partner and I are circling our arms to the inside. There are all sorts of circular configurations you can use for this drill.

The next drill deals with neutralization. I have three specific actions I teach my students. Here you neutralize your opponent's oncoming force and off balance him or her. Drills #1&2 you rotate without stepping. Drill #3 you step back to aid your neutralization.

#1

#2

#3

The next drill is blind trapping. You use the sensitivity gained from 6 stroke to continually counter trap your partner's block.

I punch. She parries. I fold my elbow and grab her wrist with my other hand. (continued on next page)

Blind trapping continued

She blocks my punch. I thread my left hand in to remove her hand and palm punch. She deflects.

I slap her arm down and palm strike. She deflects it. I fold my elbow, grab her wrist, and backfist strike. You can see how this can go on and on with her blocking my strikes and I counter trap her blocking actions, setting her up for another strike.

Blind locking is doing the preceding drill but using touch sensitivity to turn her defense into a joint locking action.

I punch. She deflects. Feeling her palm on my arm, I trap it and roll my elbow over...

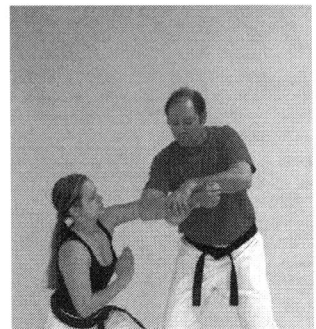   

...for a center lock. I release and punch. She deflects. I catch her deflecting arm and go into an arm bar.

Blind locking continued

I release and punch. She deflects. I grab her fingers and turn it into a full finger lock.

What is the connection of monitoring to reaction time? I hear a lot about this term, "reaction time," and I want to go over it in a different light. To me, reaction time is a myth. Let's look at it. This is my definition of reaction time:

REACTION TIME IS THE TIME IT TAKES TO GO FROM UNPREPARED TO RESPONSE. Reaction time is how fast you react to any given thing. Here's the catch; to "react" you have to be somewhat unaware of it or some part of it to begin with. Surprise enters into it. You are prodded into action by a stimulus. There is the fault in the thinking. For your reaction time to be off it has to be slower than you need it to be. Slow and fast are mistakes in timing. Timing is based on observation (monitoring) and preparation (positioning). So, for one to have "slow reaction time," either observation is out or preparation is out or both are out. Somebody does a move. Your observation of it is late, even by a hair. You go, "Oops." You do the defense or counter move. You feel you have a slow "reaction time." The photos below show me getting hit because I wasn't paying attention.

Let me give you an actual example of how observation and preparation are the key points here to timing. I was having a student doing a timing drill. He was going to hit his partner when his partner stopped moving. The student was late and couldn't figure out why and I overheard the term "reaction time." I just supposed that this was being given as the reason. I pointed out that since the apparancy of time is the movement of things through a given space, I asked when did he launch? Keep in mind that when anybody stops there is a *beginning* of the stopping action, the actual slowing down and then the final halting. This may take 1/4 of a second but it will still go through these three distinct phases.

His answer was "at the end of the stop." My reply was that his partner is *done* stopping by that time and he will go on to something else. The realization came instantly. I gave a demonstration by having an Orange belt hit me at the beginning of my stop. I checked with my student later. The "reaction time" had improved. What had occurred was observation became more acute and the preparation occurred sooner. He developed a *response time.* I illustrate this on the next page. So, when you look at it, if you have slow "reaction time," you will never be able to fix it because that's not getting to the root of the matter. Get in your observation, be prepared, and you will see and be able to handle all sorts of things you never have before.

"Slow reaction time" - She waits until I'm done with my attack before she counters.

She counter strikes right at the beginning of the end of my action. Her strike lands sooner = "quicker reaction time."

Here is another method of monitoring that I don't use but is an interesting one. A martial arts compadre of mine, Fred King, uses this method. He will watch for his opponent's energy "spikes" and drops. What he is looking at here is when an opponent is going from a preparation or stance to launching the attack his energy level will rise, often dramatically. He watches for this spike in energy. When he perceives the spike, he goes on the defense. He'll will look for an energy lapse or drop. This is when he'll go on the offense. I can see where he is coming from with this. This is a different way of observing your opponent but it *is* observing your opponent and that is the underlying point in monitoring – observation.

Fred's comments on the above are this: *"re: my "obs" (observation) when the person spikes I might jam too. It's not always defensive. Depends. If he starts to RAMP UP the energy and I can spot it as it ramps I'll go after him as he's "ramping" while I'm hitting him, typically with a backfist. He's in the prep mode. There's always "time associated with the spike" unless they are like you and the spike typically is at THE SAME TIME as the action, which is quite unusual. Ray McCallum use to ramp, Letuli ramped - doesn't mean I was fast enough to move on them but I typically 'saw it coming.'"*

I am ramped up and then drop energy. She kicks me during the energy drop.

I ramp up. Right when my partner sees the energy spike, he hits me. The key here is to hit me when I begin.

Monitoring also comes into play in two other areas: *recognition of your own positioning* and *spotting your opponent's position* (chapter 5 in this book).

Personal monitoring is awareness of self, awareness of your own positioning at any given time. An easy way to look at this is how many times have you begun to throw a kick and gotten hit in the face by your opponent? You didn't know it at the time but when you threw the kick, you dropped your hands. Or you keep getting hit in the face by your opponent and you don't see that your lead hand has a tendency to drift off to your left side opening yourself up for his jab. Or one of many mistakes you make but don't see yourself making.

She doesn't notice that she flails her arms when she kicks. I take advantage of this and hit her right when she begins.

He doesn't see his lead hand drift to the side. I take advantage of it by hitting him when it does.

Quite often a beginner will have too much attention on what he is doing, whether it is what he is going to do to his opponent or his anxiety on *"what the heck am I going to do now?"* This isn't personal monitoring but tunnel vision. To handle this, I teach to monitor your partner first and then to monitor yourself. To keep the pendulum from swinging too far the other way (monitoring him to only monitoring yourself), I'll tell my students to *"include your opponent in the equation."*

The point I make here is that monitoring isn't only attack recognition. It is getting your awareness out over the entire situation so that you don't have any stuck attention on your opponent, and stuck attention on yourself and so forth. This is a fairly advanced stage of awareness when you are cognizant of your opponent <u>and of yourself</u> at the same time without being overly out of balance in one direction or another. This is what I mean. I don't claim it to be easy to start out with but with drilling and understanding of it, it can be done.

Whenever you get the opportunity to observe a true master in action like the late Prof. Presas, Prof. Wally Jay, or Sensei Teruo Chinen, you'll notice that they are very aware of both the opponent and themselves so that their actions work off of the moves of their opponent. I feel this is what Bruce Lee meant by his opponent's action becomes his action. This is monitoring at its highest stage.

Monitoring. This is the most important principle in American Freestyle Karate. All other principles depend on your monitoring skill.
- Your timing will be off if you can't spot your opponent comfortably.
- Your distancing will be inaccurate for the same reason.
- Your balance and positioning will be off if you can't monitor yourself.
- Your mobility will be inefficient if your balance and positioning aren't right and
- you won't even be able to spot that if you can't monitor yourself.

As I said, monitoring is the key to the rest of the principles.

2. TIMING

sub-principle: "When" is more important than how fast.

Timing is number two on my list. It is ever so slightly more important than distancing although the two are almost interchangeable in importance to me. The first and principle key flaw in people's timing is that they have no working definition for it. I have asked many students and instructors at my seminars and have *never* gotten the same answer yet. Here is my working definition for it:

TIMING IS A <u>DECISION OF WHEN</u>.

When what? When anything. The mistakes made in timing have to do with the *when* of things, not the speed of them. The mistakes of timing are only two: too early or too late, not too fast or slow but too early or too late. Everyone knows timing in every day life. Whether you are driving on the freeway, drinking a cup of coffee or going to work. Everyone knows timing. My best example has to do with eating dinner. As a kid you know that dinner time is 6:00 PM. If you get there too early, you have to help set the table. If you get there too late, you miss out on dinner and you end up doing the dishes for being late. You get there on time and dinner is served.

Offensive Timing - Look at this regarding your attacks. If your attack is too late, your opponent is out of the way or is now guarded or something like that. If you throw it too early then you miss the target and now have alerted them to your intentions. *"When is the right time to throw my attacks?"* The best time to throw an attack is when your opponent is not prepared for it, when he is out of position. So, when is that?

When your opponent squares off to spar/fight you, he is prepared to some degree. He expects some sort of resistance from you so, to that degree, he's aware of you. The trick is to get him to be less aware of you. You get him to change his position.

squared off

position change

attack

As he changes his position he will have at the very least some attention (consciously or subconsciously) on his change which means some of his attention comes off of you. Your trigger is that point of change. That is the time to attack. His change can be a change in stance, in his direction of movement, in a reaction to a fake, all sorts of places.

Here are a number of changes of your opponent that you can trigger your attack or defense off of. These are not, by any means, all of them.
1. during his stance change/weight shift
2. during his footwork
3. during his hand position change
4. during his advance
5. during his retreat
6. during his reaction to a fake
7. when he comes to a halt or stand still

Offensive timing #1 - during his stance change or weight shift

Offensive timing #2 - during his footwork

Offensive timing #3 - during his hand position change

Offensive timing #4 - during his advance (note: this particular example could be looked at as either offensive or defensive. If I stand still, it is defensive. If I lunge forward, it is offensive)

Offensive timing #5 - during his retreat

Offensive timing #6 - during his reaction to a fake

Offensive timing #7 - when he comes to a halt or stand still

That simplicity is the essence to offensive timing. Attack him when he is less or least ready for you. Again, I mention that the key mistakes in timing are *too soon* and *too late*. There is a hidden mistake in timing as well. This is preparation to move.

The Hidden Mistake
The second principal key flaw in timing has to do with preparation. I will teach the above drills in seminars and then will ask the students, *"Who feels they are still having trouble with their timing?"* I will have whoever has trouble execute the timing drill again. I tell the others to watch closely and tell me what the first motion does. Hardly anyone ever spots the mistake. Invariably, one for one, the student who is having trouble with his timing *is bending his knees first* and then moving. In other words, he is wasting his split second *getting ready to move* instead of moving. When that was corrected there were no more timing problems.

She's unprepared with her legs being straight. She sees my arm drop, prepares to move and then moves = late arrival.

With her legs bent, she's now prepared to move right when she see's my change in position.

One area regarding your timing you might look at is in coordinating your attack with your entry footwork. Too often an attack will come in out of synchronization with your footwork. You get there and haven't thrown it (too late) or you throw it too soon without having gotten there (too soon). You will need to time your attack so that you are hitting right when you get into range of the particular hit you're doing (i.e. side kick, back fist etc.). Often you'll have to begin your attack mid range cross/mid step so that lands when you get there. The bottom photo sequence shows your strike starting too late.

she starts...

...she arrives...

if your partner is on guard, you will get hit on your way in

...and punches

In this example the attack is coming too soon and is nowhere near the target.

What is called initial move helps handle this. The way I teach this concept of initial move is to throw your attack or fake just as the lead foot moves, not after. This gets something going forward at your opponent as you go forward at your opponent. A mistake is to go forward at your opponent without throwing something at him as you do so. He can hit you as you come in if you give him nothing to occupy his attention with. My motto here is If you don't give him something to do, he'll give you something to do. Exceptions to this are when you are, as a tactic, moving in at a measured entry speed and blocking what he throws at you (aggressive defense) or creeping into range. All other attack modes, however, you apply initial move to.

This is an example I use with my students all the time. It is as though my partner has a rope or belt tied around my wrist and ankle and then yanks. It gets across the idea of hand and foot moving at the same time.

An excellent example of initial move is the lunge low round kick. This is a technique I was well known for. Your kicking foot *and* your hips move forward at the same time. Your rear foot pulls up as your kick lands. This is a great attack for someone who is inadvertently too close to you. Make sure that your hips move forward and not to lean back before firing the kick.

Defensive timing is just as simple. Offensive and defensive timing both hinge on change. Your opponent starts (hopefully) out of range. Well, in order to hit you he has to come in at you. That is a change in position in space, from farther to closer. If you are going to evade by angling or backing up, that is the time to do it. If your timing is acute you can wait till the last instant and make him miss by a hair. If you are going to block, then start your blocking action as he starts his attack so that you intercept the attack. Note: some people prefer to block or cover the target at the last possible instant "catch" it like a baseball catcher. The timing on that is extremely tight. Either way you're going off of a change in your opponent from no offense to an offensive action. My good friend, Robert Edwards of Tacoma, Washington is a master of this.

When your opponent is out of range, he will have to cover distance to land his attack.

The "Robert Edwards Catch" - Handling the attack at the last possible moment.

Note: You're going to have to develop your Monitoring in order to develop split second timing. That will be essential. It will be hard to determine when if you don't know what or where to spot in the first place. Timing is a decision of when. Offensive timing is your decision of when to attack. Defensive timing is your spotting of their decision of when to attack and your "when" of handling it.

Where does speed play into this? Speed is an attribute. I don't worry much about the development of speed. Everybody has a certain miles per hour speed they can attain and can work at going even faster if they train to do so. Application of monitoring, timing, and distancing can nullify speed. Speed is a physical/mechanical attribute and not up into the realm of principles. You should work to develop your timing to match the speed you have, not develop your speed because your timing is poor. This statement does not negate the need for developing speedy techniques. By all means, develop speed in all your actions so that you have great speed and timing. Just don't work on speed alone. A great drill to develop timing is to choose any move you want to sharpen your timing on and get in front of a television set. Put an action movie on. When the scene changes from one shot to another, do your move right on the change. Not before or after. Do it right on the change. You'll notice that it'll take great concentration at first. As you get better at it you'll become more relaxed and your timing, your when, will get better. You can do this with any offensive or defensive move. Remember, <u>too soon</u> and <u>too late</u> are the mistakes of timing, not too fast or too slow. And keep in mind that the cornerstone of timing is monitoring.

3. DISTANCING

sub-principle: How close you are will determine what you can and cannot do. corollary: the closer your opponent is to you, the harder it is to defend.

Distancing is next on the list of important principles in my consideration. The proper range for any given situation is the one which will yield results. It all depends upon the results you wish to have.

It is good to know the definition of the word *range:*
1. *distance between a weapon and a target,*
2. *(military) the farthest distance at which something can operate effectively, e.g. the farthest to which a gun can shoot a bullet.*

That's simple. This is a workable definition that covers all types of weapons, whether in the unarmed or armed martial arts. A good system of deciding distancing, in my opinion, is another of the deficiencies in modern day martial arts. Many groups operate off of *some* kind of defined critical distance. Often offensive distancing differs from defensive distancing. Usually critical distance is defined in terms of your *effective hitting range*, the closest you can get so you don't have to travel very far (or work very hard) in order to hit your opponent. This, however, works both ways and puts you in danger as well.

My concept of critical distance is a defensive one – personal safety comes first. *Critical Distance Line* (CDL) - Offensively and defensively, the closest you can get to your opponent and still be safe (in my opinion) is where *he can just touch you with his rear leg front kick - just enough to dirty your shirt but not enough to get a decent impact.*

Nicole sets her CDL for Pem (1-3). This is the distance where she is just touched by him. It, however, is unsuitable for me as I have longer legs than Pem (4). She resets her CDL for my length of legs (5-6). Your CDL will vary from person to person, no matter how minor the variation.

Beyond Kick & Punch - The Complete Fighting Principles Of American Freestyle Karate

The rear leg front kick is the fastest long range, yet least telegraphed attack a person can throw. A rear leg round kick, side kick, and spin kick all have longer reach but are more telegraphed. The back leg front kick can be fired with the least telegraphed body motion. So, you stay a hair away from penetrating impact of that kick. This distance will make it necessary for your opponent to take some sort of big action involving footwork in order to attack you. In effect he will have to move his whole body, not just a body part. He will have to move the entire body to get to you and that will be enough of a telegraph for you to spot if your monitoring is there. This is also explained in the section on Monitoring as the Critical Distance Line (CDL).

front kick

round kick

side kick

The above photo sequences show the differences between the telltale body motion inherent in front kick, round kick, and side kick. The round and side kicks require more motion to execute, therefore, they are easier to see coming.

Your opponent will want to stand however close or far away from you as he feels comfortable. This can present problems to your offense IF you do not recognize exactly what range he is at. He may stand closer or father away than what is optimum for you. If you can't manipulate the range, then it is best for you to know how to operate and attack from each. So, I break down range and what footwork to apply when you attack. The following is a bulletin from an in-house manual for my students.

FOOTWORK BY RANGE

This is a list of the different types of footwork you can use at the 4 different ranges of sparring. The objectives of learning these are to be able to recognize which range you are in at any given moment and to get out of using inappropriate methods of entry for the range you are at.

Offensively the aim for you is to not get stuck into doing only one kind of range so that when your opponent tries this on you, so what. You'll be able to work from wherever they go. This will even mess them up more.

OUT OF RANGE - "Long" footwork. Step-slide up, step-step roll, slide up-lunge, slide up-step through (and reverse), step through-lunge. These steps aren't speed steps but even rhythm steps. Using a flow to move in from long range will enable you to change up or defend yourself when you come in, if necessary. The idea here is that when your opponent is outside of the CDL you will usually have to compound (double, triple, etc.) your footwork in order to reach your opponent. Even more important, you will have to correctly estimate the distance you will have to cover and how to cover it. Outside of range is where you will use your slower and more flowing types of entry.

Step-slide round kick

Step-step roll side kick

Slide up-lunge

Step-step roll side kick

Slide up-lunge

CRITICAL DISTANCE LINE/FIRING LINE - On the CDL is where you will use your normal footwork; your slide up, step through, spin kicks and so forth. Here you can either take off full speed or measure the speed of your entry footwork. This is the optimum distance for your defense, close enough to entice them into making a mistake but far enough off so that you don't fall into their trap.

Slide up

Step through

Spinning kick

INSIDE FIRING LINE - Lunge kick or punch, skip kick or punch. On the Inside Firing Line you are a hair within their attacking range so explosive speed type takeoffs are required. Your lunge and skip kicks that don't take that much movement to execute are your best bets. You will also have to throw your attacks right at the same time as your footwork. Since your are inside of their hitting range you need to make your action as quick as possible to reduce the chance of your getting hit. (illustrated next page)

Beyond Kick & Punch - The Complete Fighting Principles Of American Freestyle Karate

Lunge

Skip kick - the dropping of the rear leg and the pick up of the front leg are done simultaneously.

LEANING TOUCH RANGE - (Where you can lean forward and touch your partner). Upper body explosion. At Leaning Touch Range you can use an explosive upper body take off for your entry action and let your feet follow your move. This is what a lot of tournament players use today but at the wrong range. When you are close enough to catch your opponent by surprise it is a great take off but when your opponent knows how to keep range, then you don't use this one.

too close to my partner

With Inside Firing Line and Leaning Touch Range you take off at full speed. You are inside the Critical Distance Line so you are in potential danger. At this range it is difficult for your opponent to react/respond quick enough. These are good for when you sneak into range or if your opponent inadvertently crosses into your range of hitting. The idea is to become familiar with the different ranges and then to become skilled at the footwork needed at each range. This way you won't ever be stuck if your opponent keeps a different distance than the one you prefer.

You can manipulate your offensive distancing by the use of what I call "creep steps." These are ways to cross into range that are hidden from your opponent.

This is nicknamed "The Montgomery Step" after Randy Mongomery. You draw your lead foot back and come in sideways with your rear foot. The key here is to leave your upper body back so your opponent doesn't see that your foot has gotten closer. Below is a variation of this where your toes point at your opponent. This one is the "Switch Step."

Beyond Kick & Punch - The Complete Fighting Principles Of American Freestyle Karate

This is the "Toe Grip." Sitting in a low stance I use my toes to creep in across the Critical Distance Line. As I do so, I keep my upper body back to disguise the change in distancing.

This one is the "Hidden Slide." You draw your back foot up from a wide stance to prepare yourself for a lunge action. You can see by looking at the photos to the right that if you bend your knees enough and slide your back leg right behind your front one, the action is hidden. Ensure that you keep your upper body immobile as you do this.

I call this the "Leaning Horse Stance." Sitting very deep in Horse stance, you lean your upper body back to give the appearance of increased distance between the two of you. Your lead foot slips in over the Critical Distance Line to get the range for your backfist strike.

One more thing to offensive distancing is the knowledge of the range of your own attacking weapons, how long your side kick is, how long your punch is, etc. When you cross the range you need to know how close you have to get to them in order to land a telling blow with whatever weapon you are using. Most karate people are usually pretty good at this.

(side note: To ensure that my students are versed at all ranges, I teach them a number of close in techniques as part of a series of punch and kick combinations. The close in range is one of the weakest areas I find in modern day karate fighters. In my school these are punch combinations 11-15 and kick combinations 11-15.)

Punch combination 11 - Left uppercut to the liver, right uppercut to the spleen, left hook to the jaw.

Punch combination 12 - Left hook to the floating ribs, left hook to the temple.

Punch combination 13 - Right uppercut to the chin, left hook to the jaw, short straight right to the jaw

Punch combination 14 - Double lead uppercut (midsection and chin), short straight right to the jaw.

Punch combination 15 - Palm slap to the ear, upward palm to the groin (note: your can reverse the targets in this one).

It is important to become comfortable with the inside range. This is a range which can be neglected in modern day karate training. Most karate blows impact at an extended range, whether kick or punch. Going inside and hitting is more of a boxing tactic than an oriental martial arts move yet here is where a number of fights actually end up at. To develop comfort in this range it is important to start out slowly so that you can get used to someone being inside your comfort zone. Training in this range you will also need to be willing to get hit. There is no way to avoid it when you are in this close.

Kick combination 11 - Shin kick, "Thai" kick (round kick with the shin to your opponent's thigh).

Kick combination 12 - Double shin kick (delivered in a shuffle/switch step fashion).

Kick combination 13 - (from a clinch) Two alternating inside foot sweeps, groin kick.

Kick combination 14 - Knee to the floating ribs, stomp down on the foot.

Kick combination 15 - Forward knee to the thigh, follow up shin kick.

Defensively you can use this knowledge to foil your opponent's main method of entry. Usually a person will find a range he is comfortable at and then try to launch all of their attacks from that degree of closeness. When you understand exactly what types of footwork are effective from the different ranges, then you can expect the type of footwork your opponent is trying to set up for. Then you can adjust and go to a range that isn't suitable for that footwork. In other words you mess up his attack without even touching him. The different types of defensive footwork are covered in the chapter on Mobility.

Defensive distancing gets into an interesting game. You see, almost every fighter has a "CDL" that he favors, a distance he feels comfortable at. What you need to do is to spot which of the preceding 4 ranges his favorite is and then *deny him that range*. You can *deny him that range* before he ever gets set or move just as he moves. Example 1 (below): A hand fighter who likes to creep up on the inside firing line. Just as he gets to that point you take one step back and nail him with a counter kick. Example 2 (below): A kicker who likes to stay outside of range and then lunge in and kick you. You can stalk him and press him and never let him get the distance away from you that he wants.

His denying you the distance *you want* doesn't necessarily put you out of being cause over the situation. Knowledge of the 4 distances outlined above and the appropriate footworks for each will give you the options you need. Drill these and you will be able to operate at any distance.

A brilliant example of a fighter commanding range is in the first Muhammed Ali – Sonny Liston fight. Ali kept Liston out of his power range the whole fight. Ali never let Sonny hit him with power shots because he controlled the distancing. This was one of Muhammed Ali's greatest assets.

Another defensive use to recognition of ranges is to know that your opponent will have to use a certain category of footwork to cover their range. That will let you know what to expect when they take off at you from where they are. If he is close to you, expect an explosive take off. The farther away he is, the bigger the motion he will have to use to get to you. It becomes very simple when you have the tools. Knowledge of range is one of your most important tools. If you monitor the actions of your opponent, use timing, and can figure out what distance your opponent likes to use (or the one you want to use along with the most efficient footwork), you will have an unbeatable trio. The types of defensive footwork to control distance will be covered in the chapter on Mobility.

Ali using his leaning defense against Liston

Muhammed Ali keeping Sonny Liston at bay with his long jab.

4. BALANCE

sub-principle: If you are familiar with everything, you will be surprised by nothing.

"Secret Fighting Arts Of The World" is a book written by Robert W. Smith and a number of friends under the pseudonym of John F. Gilbey. It was done as of a parody of all the secrets of fighting arts kinds of books coming out in the mid-1960s. The funny thing about this book is that if you actually read it, it contained a good number of nuggets of fighting wisdom. One chapter that affected me was the one on surprise called *"The Unexpected Tactic."* The fighter in the chapter bragged about how he had defeated a number of other fighters by doing the unexpected. This led me to develop my own balance so that I would not be surprised by the unexpected.

Balance is a very neglected portion of many martial artists training. I don't mean only equilibrium. I mean an equality of action along with equilibrium. I divide balance up into 5 sections:
1) left and right side balance
2) top and bottom balance (hands and feet)
3) offensive and defensive actions
4) mobility and immobility
5) equilibrium.

The first 4 are the sadly neglected ones in today's training.

1. *Left/right* balance is better these days but no fighter is truly skilled unless they can back up their naturally coordinated side with the other side. Originally, karate players used their front hand for blocking and the rear hand for hitting. Then, in about the middle 1960s, Chuck Norris became the first player to utilize both sides of his body in competition and he virtually defeated everybody. Shortly after that Bruce Lee came out with the idea of using your coordinated side as your front footed side and your power side. After that, Bill Wallace became famous for being able to hit anyone with only his left (front) leg. Joe Lewis also favored his lead side for hitting. This has led a lot of people in the U.S. to follow suit. That has led players to become out of balance.

I first realized the importance of left/right balance when I was competing in Tacoma, Washington watching two heavyweights fight. They were both right hand punchers. They each grabbed the others right sleeve with their own right hand and then tried to free themselves while keeping a hold of the other. Picture one fishing line with a hook at either end and a fish caught on each hook. It was fascinating.

No usage of the left hand here = two fish caught on the same line.

In 1972 I broke one of the bones in my right hand at a karate tournament. The importance of balance personally hit home. Two weeks later I was fighting Byong Yu at the International Karate Championships for the lightweight championship. The overtime went on for 19 minutes until I decided to counter punch him with my left hand as he came in. I waited till he moved. He moved. I began to fire. He hit me with his punch before mine even left its chamber. That's what I got for only being right handed. Since then I now can block, kick, and punch from either side with either hand or foot. It's a lot of work but if I can do it, so can you. When you can do right and left side, you will not be caught unprepared by someone who can. I give many examples of left-right balance in chapter 7 when I detail a number of combinations I teach in my school.

2. *Top/bottom* balance is one of those things where many players have been misled. *"Oh I'm sorry but you're definitely not a kicker"* or *"With legs like those you don't need to develop you hands."* These are mistaken ways of thinking. One doesn't need to be a flashy, high-flying kicker in order to be a skilled kicker. That's tournament karate attitude. It may sound funny my saying this because, after all, I have spent a lot of time developing my own kicking ability. In my opinion a person doesn't need to be a "marvelous" kicker in order to become a skilled kicker. Flash isn't necessarily *efficient skill*. A skilled kicker is one who *can hit you* with his kicks, period. As for being a great kicker who doesn't need to develop hands, good luck. Someone will always be able to get inside your kick or extend the distance and make you miss as in the example below.

A personal example of this is I flunked my black belt test twice before finally making it. The second time I took my black belt test my instructor had me spar this guy who was short, strong, and could take a good shot. I had pressured my teacher into letting me test it so he put me up against the absolutely worst guy for me to spar against. I'd hit him with a kick and he'd go through it like it didn't even touch him and hit me with 10-15 punches. This would go on over and over, same pattern. You see, I couldn't use my hands to save my life let alone my belt test. He put me against a hand fighter who would disregard my kick and multiple punch. Needless to say I flunked that one. After that I began to develop my hands along with my kicks.

Now I find that experience funny because I have defeated more opponents because of that one aspect alone. If he was a good kicker, I would cut off his kicks and hit him with my hands. If he only punched, I would stay away and kick him. The same with the LEFT/RIGHT balance factor. I could shut off his good side and nail him.

Develop this or a good fighter will take advantage of it on you. I detail 10 of what I call the hand and foot combinations in chapter 7 to develop top-bottom balance.

3. *Offensive/defensive* balance is a hard one to get through to a lot of students. They are either naturally aggressive or non-aggressive. The catch is that if you wait for your opponent to come to you so that you can handle him with your defense and he has the same idea in mind, nothing gets done. Or if you are very aggressive, you and your opponent will be battering rams to each other. Even if you win, you are going to get beat up to some degree. It is better to develop both sides of the game, offense and defense so that you don't get stuck.

To educate a passive person in offensive approaches you can devise drills based off of the 5 approaches of attack outlined in my first book on sparring, **American Freestyle Karate: A Guide To Sparring**. They are explained well enough there so that I only go briefly over them in chapter 7. The defensive approaches should be drilled into an aggressive person just based on this fact alone: someone out there, somewhere, is bigger, stronger, and meaner than you and you might actually meet them some day. And when you do you better be prepared.

Once you have gotten to where you can both mount an offense and defense, you can begin getting into a true skill which is to be able to shift from one to the other instantly. This is another major missing piece of the overall pie in most karate players fighting ability. This is why an overly aggressive fighter can get hit by a good counter attacker and also why a defensive minded person can get overrun by a good offensive fighter.

You should be able to shift, in mid movement from offensive to defensive mode. You attack, they counter, you handle their counter. If you want to continue the attack after that, fine. I've seen many fighters taking a shot in the middle of their offense because of their inability to shift.

You should be able to defend and instantly return fire. Your opponent attacks, you block or angle, you counter attack. With most karate players, most defensive action ends with getting out of range and breaking connection with the attacker instead of mounting a counter offense of their own.

The pinnacle of offensive/defensive balance is to be able to shift instantly from one to the other. Your monitoring, timing, and positioning have to be spot on but as with the others, it can be done.

Defending yourself mid a combination attack. This is a skill that I developed for myself that proved useful time and time again. Most karate fighters prefer to fight on through the counter attack. This is fine if you are facing a weak opponent. I never take for granted that my opponent is weak.

Changing from defense to counter offense is more prevalent in modern day karate. The key to being truly effective with this is to go off of a "touch trigger." The moment your defense touches you counter fire.

4. *Mobility/immobility* balance is usually neglected because of the viewpoint of whatever style is being taught. Japanese styles mostly push having a power base and mobility ruins that base. A lot of tournament players like to be mobile because to sit still makes them an easy target to hit. Neither side is right or wrong. Yes, sitting still will make you a better target. And yes, you won't be rooted when you hit if you're moving all over the place. What to remember is that there is a time for moving around and a time for planting yourself. It's if you're only one or the other (a mover or a planter), you can be taken advantage of by a smarter fighter.

One of the main advantages to being mobile is that it will hide your initial movement to your take off. It also makes you a harder target to hit. Advantages to being rooted is that you will have less of a tendency to go out of equilibrium and it does make your blocking stronger and builds your confront. The main thing is to be able to be comfortable with both so that when faced with one or the other you will not be taken off guard. You must be able to shift from one to the other so that when you want to move, you can and when you want to plant, you can. I can't get much plainer than that. (note: I detail a number of footwork set ups in chapters 5&6 which will enhance your mobility.)

5. *Equilibrium* is basically keeping from falling over and how well you can accomplish that. There are two main points to maintaining your equilibrium: A) keeping control of your center of gravity and B) knowing how and when to counter balance yourself.

By bending your knees, lowering your hips, and keeping your back straight you can keep your center of gravity low. This is a basic for many martial arts. Don't let your hips get too high or else you're easily toppled or put off balance.

standing too high   *workable stance for balance*   *standing too low*

When you're moving it is harder to keep your hips low so mainly keep your upper body centered over your hips and your knees bent as you move. To maintain structural equilibrium, stay relatively straight up and down. Keeping from leaning while you move will keep you from losing your balance in one direction or another. I tell my students that when they move to get the feeling that they are being pulled around by their belt. This gives a good picture of leading with the hips when moving. It's hard to do when you're used to all sorts of upper body take-offs but it's safer and you are in a position to hit harder when you do. Note: I do cheat on this when I am in Leaning Touch Range because it's almost a sure bet that I will hit my opponent from that range and I can use their body to stop my forward momentum.

You see in the above photo series how my partner pulls me forward by my belt. This is the manner to move forward so that you don't end up leaning your shoulders in towards your opponent. You can run into a punch to the face if you do that. To do this, you need to "think with the hips." When I teach children I use the visual idea of punching someone in the belly with the knot of your belt. That gets the idea across. For adults I'll use the same idea as well as telling them to move forward as though they were moving on ice.

A very simple concept I use to describe balance is the *"three cardboard box rule."* If you take three cardboard boxes of equal dimensions (example: three feet wide by three feet tall) and stack them exactly one on top of another, they will be stably upright. This aligns with three points of the body; the knees, the hips, and the upper torso. Take a look at anyone standing and you will see that their body structure is aligned so that one "cardboard box" is on top of another and so on.

the three cardboard box rule

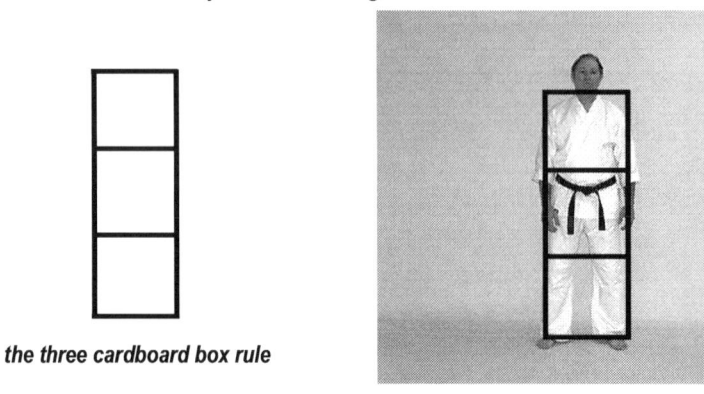

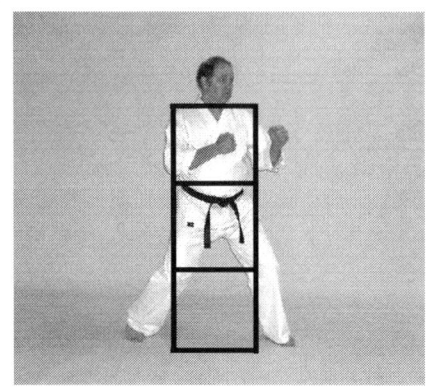

If you put any of the boxes out of vertical alignment with the others, the stack will not be as stable and will topple more easily. If you put two of the boxes out of alignment, the stack is even less stable. If you apply this to the body, all you need to do is ruin the integrity of the structure of the body, that is to say, get at least one of the three main sections out of alignment with the other sections and you will have an off balance situation. Your equilibrium will be jeopardized.

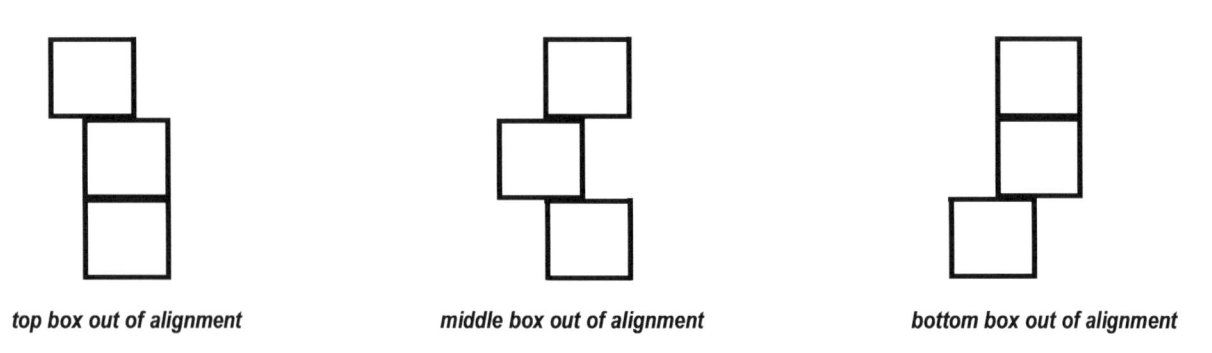

top box out of alignment **middle box out of alignment** **bottom box out of alignment**

So to maintain standing equilibrium, I stress the importance of not getting the body out of structural alignment. I keep the "three cardboard boxes" one atop the other. For sweeping and throwing techniques, I'll work on getting the "three cardboard boxes" *out of alignment* with the others.

By superimposing the boxes on the photos, you can see what I mean by getting one box out of alignment with the others.

Beyond Kick & Punch - The Complete Fighting Principles Of American Freestyle Karate

I push his upper body as I advance for the sweep. With the "upper box" out of alignment his leg is easier to sweep.

Beyond Kick & Punch - The Complete Fighting Principles Of American Freestyle Karate

A key point about the knee roll is that you insert your knee as far behind his knee as possible. This way when you roll his knee, the pressure will come from behind his knee. His upper body will rotate to the side as you do so and actually dislodge two "boxes."

With the two hand shoulder throw, I jam my hips into his while holding his lapel firmly. This pushes his hips backwards, forcing his upper body to bend forward.

Counter balancing is used chiefly in kicking. The idea is this. When you stick your leg outward from your body, the weight of it will pull your body in that direction. In order to offset that pull you lean your body in the opposite direction so that you will not fall during the kicking action. If you look at pictures of Bill Wallace he is leaning over so that his body is virtually sideways ... and he is fantastically limber. This is how you set yourself up for multiple kicks. You counter balance the weight of your leg with your upper body.

With no counter balance, you will begin to fall toward the direction of your outstretched leg.

I use the three cardboard box rule in counter balancing for kicking as well. The key here is to not get any part of the body out of straight alignment with the others. A straight line between the kicking foot (going up through the leg, hips, waist, and torso) head is essential for balancing while kicking. Bend your waist at the *side,* not through the *belly* to maintain your straight line. You stack the three cardboard boxes and then lean them. If the middle or top box is out of alignment, you'll jeopardize your balance. If you bend at the belly or bend your neck to look under your lead shoulder (instead of over the top of it) you will pull yourself off balance during the kick.

The body is now counter balanced.    *The above kick shows good alignment.*    *The above kick is out of alignment.*

Recognition of where or how your opponent is out of balance is quite a weapon in your arsenal. Almost everyone is out of balance in some area or another. One fighter might be a fantastic kicker but only with one leg. Another might be great with his hands but never moves much. Yet another's offensive skills may be very good but he has no defense. You see what I mean? A brilliant example of exploiting lack of balance is when Buster Douglas knocked out Mike Tyson for the heavyweight title. Tyson was considered unbeatable. Douglas found the flaw in Tyson's fight game. Tyson had no defense. He usually had his opponents scared of his formidable punching power. They had lost before they even got into the ring. Douglas cut off Tyson's punching power by tying him up in the clinches and then later hit him with crisp, sharp punches. Tyson just ate the punches and that led to his being knocked out. By being a one-dimensional fighter (not balanced), Mike Tyson lost his crown.

You can exploit out of balance in two fashions: work towards their weak side or shut off their strong side. The nice thing is that often many fighters fail to recognize their own out of balance points or they think they can over compensate with their strong points anyway. I've only met a couple people who could do that. Bill Wallace was one of them. He was one of a handful of fighters would could make his opponents fight within *his* framework or parameters. The rest of us are stuck with our faults.

In the above sequence I can see he favors his right hand over his left. I angle to his weak side (the left) and attack from there.

Seeing his right hand ready to fire, I cut off his avenue of attack simply by putting my hand in front of his. Surprisingly enough, this works more often than not.

I am a strong believer of balance because it is one thing I have consistently exploited in others in my competition career. I have been able to spot what a persons strong points and weak points within seconds while sparring them. I have also worked on my own balance so that I don't get caught because of having the same limitations. To further illustrate this, I've included two bulletins give to my own students.

MIX AND MATCH - BLACK BELT STRATEGY

Mix and match is a term I started using for the younger students to get the idea of putting together combinations and fakes, angles and blocks and counters. The idea is instead of doing only one thing you mix them all up.

Mix and match for an adult is a little different. The concept is to mix up your direct and indirect offenses and defenses and match them up to your particular opponents weakness. If you stick to any one part of fighting you become limited and your limitation can be found and exploited. Becoming skilled at balance can prevent this. In sparring how does one find and then exploit their opponent's weakness.

You need to adopt a GAME PLAN, an actual objective purpose to your sparring. In the early days of my sparring my GAME PLAN was to not get hit. I did anything (mostly run away) to avoid getting hit. Later on in my competitive career my GAME PLAN was to score first. It didn't matter if I ran, was aggressive, or whatever, just as long as I was the first guy to score. Then I went through a stage where I wanted to become balanced left and right, top and bottom so I did that as my GAME PLAN.

Now if you adopt, as a GAME PLAN, to balance your skills and approaches, that will indeed be the result. It won't necessarily easy though it needn't be excruciatingly hard either.

I did this in class one night. Drill alternating a direct offense and indirect offense, and then a direct defense and indirect defense. Then spar with a partner, again alternating the direct and indirect approaches. Then spar playing mix and match, that is to say, mix up your approaches until you find a weakness in your partner to exploit and then exploit the heck out of it. Then once they catch on, shift to something else. It worked marvelously in class. You'll end up sparring with a purpose and thinking on your feet.

LESSON FROM JAPAN

Miyamoto Musashi was the greatest swordsman in Japan. He wrote a book on strategy called, *"The Book Of Five Rings."* This is a great quote from that book which pertains to Black Belt sparring:

"The spirit of 'mountain and sea change' refers to the fact that while one is engaged in combat with an opponent, it is bad to frequently repeat the same tactic. Repeating the same tactic twice is sometimes unavoidable, but it is not to be done three times. In the process of performing a trick on the opponent, you fail once, even if you try again, you will meet with no more success than the first time. Above all, try a different approach and take the opponent by surprise. If it fails, you must try something different again. In this manner, if the opponent expects mountain, give him the sea; if he expects the sea, give him mountains. Taking people by surprise is a teaching."

This is the same passage from the Kenji Tokitsu translation (Miyamoto Musashi – His Life And Writings – Shambhala). *"Here is what I call 'the mind of the mountain and the sea.' It is harmful to do the same thing several times in the curse of combat. You can do the same thing twice but not three times. If you fail with a technique, you can begin it over again once more, but if you do not succeed this time, abruptly apply another, completely different technique. In this way, if your opponent is thinking of the mountain, you apply the sea; if he is thinking if the sea, you apply the mountain. Such is the way of strategy. You must examine this well."*

An American way of putting it would be, "If he didn't fall for it the first time, what makes you think he will fall for it the second time? Do something different."

As a side note, you can use the above passage in setting your opponent up as well. This is what I call *training my opponent*. I'll do a certain move several times to get him to now expect that move. Then I change up on him and hit him with something different. It is surprisingly simple but works like a charm.

Battling Chicago's Flem Evans in Oakland, California - 1974

5. POSITIONING

principle: If you know what you can do from any position, you will never be out of position.

Positioning is next on the list because it is an area where if you know how to read a persons position, it is like them telling you what they intend to throw at you. A person's positioning of himself *will* tell you what he has in mind to throw at you. Here is a datum you can take to the bank.

An opponent never faces off at you in a position of incompetence. He will face you in a position of strength, of comfort, of confidence.

This is the position he has been taught that is the best or one that he has worked out for himself over the years. Either way from that position you can see exactly what he is set up to throw ... if you know what to look for. Here are some tips:

1. Distance between the feet. If the spacing between his feet goes only to about one and a quarter of their shoulders width, expect a lunging or hopping kick coming off of the front leg. Any further apart and he usually will have to take some kind of set up step in order to kick and keep their balance. A front foot lunge kick action needs to come from a relatively short position.

Relatively short distance between the feet make it easy to kick off of the front leg without stepping first.

Longer distance between the feet make it necessary to step before kicking with the front leg.

2. Weight distribution. A general rule of thumb is that if a person has more weight on the front foot, he tends to be a bit more decided on his action. Quite often it is an offensive action. If he has more weight on the back foot he tends to be a little more patient and perhaps defensive. With the weight evenly distributed he can go either way. Often he hasn't made up his mind. This one of weight distribution is not set in stone as there are some fighters who are aggressive but come at you from a position where their weight is on their back leg. This is the most chancy of these tips.

Weight on the front leg   *Weight on the back leg*   *Weight evenly distributed*

3. Pointing of the hands. You wouldn't think that it is this easy but a person who likes straight punch will actually point the fist at you. The same with a back fist. I call this *aiming the gun*. The striking portion will usually be pointed right at you. This is basically a declaration of intention. You can see which hand is the "live" hand and which is the "dead" hand by which hand is actually pointing at you.

4. Pointing of the feet. For kicking, I use the pointing of the opponent's foot. A front kicker will have his kicking foot pointed at you while a round kicker will have his foot turned in somewhat. A person planning a side kick will have his foot almost, if not fully, turned sideways. This follows basic body structure. Try it for yourself. Point your toes straight forward and from that position, test which is the easiest to do: front kick, round kick or side kick. Then test the same kicks in that order with your lead foot pointing at a 45 degree angle. Then do the same with your foot edge pointing at your opponent. You'll find which kicks are easier to do from what position.

Toes facing forward indicate a front kick set up.

Toes pointed inward at an angle indicate a round kick set up.

The edge of the foot pointed at you (or toes pointing totally off to the side) indicates a side kick set up.

Remember what I said earlier, *"No one will make something hard for himself to do."* A person will tell you, via body language, what he is set up to throw.

You'll notice I keep using the term set up to throw. This is because we aren't mind readers yet. You can read your opponents body position and see what he is best set up for but you never can tell EXACTLY what they are going to do. Position reading is a game of educated guesswork. It actually works very well. Incidentally, I teach this method of reading my opponent in seminars. I'll pick someone to spar. Right after we bow in and take our positions, I'll go over to a spectator and begin telling them what my partner is going to do and what I am going to counter it with. We haven't even moved yet. My highest percentage of prediction accuracy was 100% and my lowest was 78%. My average accuracy percentage rate is around 92%. That is quite an advantage I have without a kick or punch having been fired yet. You can have that same advantage.

The Hidden Factor
Very often you'll encounter a hidden factor foiling your attempts to make your tactics work. While you're trying to spar your partner/opponent, you'll be sparring something else. In fact you might never be sparring the opponent, himself, and be sparring against everything but. What do I mean here? You might be sparring your partner's rank or attributes or attitude but never the partner himself.

Let's take rank. I've seen where a Purple Belt will spar a Blue Belt and beat him. He will evenly match against another Purple Belt and then perform less than their own ability against a Green Belt or higher. What happened? As the belt rank got higher, their confidence shrank. You see what happens? All it is, is a loss of confidence in oneself against what they suppose to be the abilities of the higher ranked person. Here's another one, sparring the attributes of the partner rank than the partner. "Oh wow! Tim's kicks are just incredible. I have such a hard time against kicks. Okay Tim, go ahead and kick me and get it over with."

An excellent example of someone not falling for this was in the mixed martial arts match between Vitor Belfort and Randy Coture. In several matches Belfort had devastated his opponents with an initial move attack, basically a lunging straight punch coming off of his right side forward. His initial speed was so explosive that he had caught his opponents flat footed with his powerful left hand and then pummeled them into submission. He had built himself up such a reputation that his nickname was "The Phenom." He looked unbeatable. Well, Coture fought the perfect game plan by circling away from Belfort's left hand and ended up clinching in tight with him, smothering it. He then battered Belfort with uppercuts until Belfort dropped and the referee stopped the fight. Before his defeat by Coture, others suffered the loss of confidence against Belfort.

How about attitude? It's the same. Do you shrink away from someone who looks or acts mean? Or do you get intimidated by someone who is an "iceman," who shows no feeling? What is happening is one can get caught up in all of the significance (what something means or should mean) of your partner and then has all that in front of his eyes like a blindfold. You now spar all the significance instead of the person in front of you.

This reminds me of a story told by Sugar Ray Robinson (the original Sugar Ray), 5 time world middleweight boxing champion. He was an amateur at the time. *"One night I noticed a tough looking kid about my size on the other team. 'Who's that?' I said to George. 'That's the boy you're fighting,' he said. 'Not me,' I said. 'What's wrong?' 'Look at him,' I said. 'His nose is all flat, there's scar tissue around his eyes. He's too tough.' 'Smitty,' he said, 'if he could fight he wouldn't look like that.' George was right. The kid couldn't fight."* (from the book, "Sugar Ray" by Sugar Ray Robinson with Dave Anderson – Signet. Personal note: If you find a copy of this book, buy it. It is one of the best books I have ever read on the subject of fighting.)

Your own personal preconceived ideas about how someone will spar or what kind of skills they should have because of a belt color can get in your way. I personally know this one very well as I have fallen prey to it many times. So, what do you do about it? A good way to start is to spar your opponents position. How is he standing? Which foot is forward? Is both of his hands up? Which zones are being protected? Is he set up to kick? How close or far is he? Each position yields opportunities for your offense. Their position will tell you of their offensive and defensive possibilities. From where they are, what can they easily do? Easily do. That's the key point. Anyone can do anything from whichever position. I doubt many people will do a flying kick from a prone position, though! Is his head open? His groin? What? Look at his position. The position of the George and Irv just might be the same. It doesn't matter that George is a Brown Belt and Irv is a Blue Belt. <u>If their positions are the same, then the openings are the same.</u>

This approach you'll have to take on faith until you experience it. It works. Everybody is open for some kind of attack and everybody is set up to do only so many things. Their position will tell the tale. So, look at and spar the position, not the belt, attributes, attitudes, or what's been said by others, just the position.

If all this worries you about how to deal with your opponent's position, here's another bulletin I give to my students regarding just that.

PULLING YOUR OPPONENT OUT OF POSITION

At Brown Belt, you begin to work on strategy and the two things you want to check your opponent for is if he is set or if he isn't set. When I look at your opponent being set, I don't mean in a stance, not moving. I mean your opponent being able to hit from his position, whether he is moving or not. If he is set up to attack you, he's set. Veteran karate fighter Joe Lewis looks to see if his opponent is in range to fire his technique and if his "guns" are aimed. If so, he's at his set point.

Here is a workable outline of how to approach your opponent.

NOT SET: Direct style attack. He isn't ready. You just go on him.

SET: Indirect attack. You pull him out of setup and then you go.

The different ways you can pull your opponent out of position are:

1. Technique fake
2. Pump (footwork and body fake)
3. Angle
4. Disconnect (back up so far that you're way out of range)
5. Creep in to get your opponent jumpy
6. Draw their fire to a certain spot
7. Take away their centerline attack.

1. Technique fake

2. Pump (footwork and body fake)

3. Angle - this creates an out of positioning for him. He will need to shift to face me.

4. Disconnect - this takes away his operable range

5. Creep in to get your opponent jumpy - this is good for an opponent who doesn't like you to be close in.

6. Draw their fire to an open spot.

7. Take away their centerline attack - this is hard to depict from a side photo view but I am tucking my lead elbow in to protect my ribs, turning my lead forearm to rest right on the center line, and placing my rear fist at my solar plexus.

These are just the ones you will be tested on. These are just examples. There are all sorts of different ways you can do this. The primary thing is if your opponent is set up, pull him out of set position and then attack. Don't go in on someone who is set unless you have unbelievable speed ... and even then it's chancy. You set him up for your attack, don't get yourself setup for their attack. Ruin his position. This is the way to approach your opponent safely. Start by seeing if your opponent is ready and then act accordingly.

When watching your opponent's positional setup, watch for your opponent to pull himself out of position also. This is very common with lower belts and careless upper belts. Often he will do the work for you by going out of position by himself.

Example of my opponent pulling himself out of position - he steps to the side to switch his forward leg. He drops his hand and is now open.

Now what are you going to do regarding your own position? Well, my viewpoint is *do you know exactly how well you can punch, kick, block, and move from any given position?* That is what you need to find out.

Let's take a look at this in regards to your favorite technique (like a rear hand straight punch). First do it from an ideal position, like how you'd do it on a heavy bag or in a form. When sparring are you anywhere close to doing it that way? If not, you're throwing it from out of position. Knowing from what positions you can throw any number of techniques will lead you to being able to work out of various positions instead of one favorite position.

What *kind of position* is your favorite position, anyway? Are you trying to attack from a defensive position? Are you trying to defend from an attacking position? Are your hands where they can be used to hit and defend? What are your percentage options as far as offense, defense, and mobility in each position you find yourself in? To me, the most balanced position is one where you can as equally as possible attack, defend, and move at the same time.

As long as you know that the position you like is a defensive position, for example, then you won't try something ineffective...like mounting an offense from it. The same would be trying to be very mobile from a low stance, or defending from an aggressive position. You will find that there will be different positions which will suit different needs and approaches. In the long run you will smoothly shift and change to the one which suits the situation best. Then you might start noticing that many of your opponents will try to do everything from one position. And that's where the fun begins.

Here is a way to use *positioning defensively*. You can utilize your monitoring skills and read what you opponent is setup to throw at you. Instead of using the guard position I teach my students, you can *deny him access to the target*. Here's an example: let's say he is set up to throw a backfist to your head. You spot the line of travel from where he is to the target and put your hand exactly in the way. I won't matter much if you extend your arm out or hold it closer to the target - you just put it in the way. Then, he has to readjust. You have taken him out of his game plan, even if only for a moment. You will be surprised how effective this is.

Example of denying access to the target - I see he is prepared for a backfist. I put my arm in the direct path of his strike.

If he shifts to regain access for his backfist, I hit him during his shift.

There is one thing to watch out for and this is a huge mistake. If you put your hand up to deny him access to your head as a target, don't then move your hand to see him better. What happens is this: you put your hand up to deny him access to your head. Then, noting that you have put your hand in your line of vision to his face, you move your hand. This opens up the very target you wanted to protect. What I have seen is that a person will move his hand so that he can see his opponent's face. To me this is odd. HIS FACE ISN'T GOING TO HIT YOU. His face should be the least of your concerns. If you are going to deny access to a target, you need to deny access and keep it denied.

He spots me moving my hand in order to see him. That gives him access to the target again.

When you deny access to a target, you can either obstruct the travel route OR cover the actual target itself. It doesn't matter. This will cause your opponent to change his operating basis, even if only for a moment, and will put you in the driver's seat. Take advantage of it.

He wants the side kick. I either deny him the travel route to the target or take away the target altogether. Either way he can't have it.

Your knowledge of positioning can defeat many an opponent or at the very least nullify their efforts. On the tournament circuit I was known for being somewhat hard to hit. The reason is that I know: 1. What others can do from the position they are in and 2. I know what I can and can't do from whatever position I'm in.

These photos are from a 1980 article in Inside Kung Fu magazine. My partner is #1 rated fighter Keith Vitali.

6. MOBILITY

sub-principle: If you master movement you will not be caught off guard by it.

Mobility isn't just moving all over the place. *It is movement with a purpose*. Preferably it is movement with several possible purposes. Understanding of the uses of mobility will give you the reasoning behind your moving so that it doesn't become just a good way of burning energy.

I divide mobility into 3 parts: footwork setups, offensive, and defensive. I will take set ups first.

Footwork set ups are using movement to offset your opponent's position so that you can attack. Simply speaking, an opponent usually positions himself so that he can attack you in a straight-line fashion. I haven't had anyone come at me in a curve in the last 38 years so I feel quite comfortable with that proposition. He may move around so as to get me out of position and then come straight at me to attack but I've never been surrounded by a single person yet.

The idea of a footwork set up is what I just described. Your opponent usually will want to attack along a straight-line entry, this being the line of movement *his body* takes. I don't care if he does a round kick or hook kick or any other kind of curved action. It doesn't matter whether he is facing full frontally, at an angle or completely side facing. *His footwork will carry his body at me in a straight-line action.* If I come at him head on, his response may not be the defensive but aggressive. He may immediately counter attack. Even if I am the attacker, I also become the target.

Even if my opponent is circling me, he will eventually cross the distance to me in a straight line.

What I want to do is take the target and put it out of line with their entry path. That is all I want to accomplish. He will readjust his position in order to get back to that straight-line entry position. You nail him during the readjustment. That is the simplicity of it. You foil his entry line up by moving off of that line. He tries to get it back and you attack him as he does. You need not try to hit him on every adjustment. You might do the 3rd one or the 5th. Go back over the section on pulling your opponent out of position. These are the footwork set ups I teach my students.

1-2 & Attack - Your lead foot crosses over and back (1-2). From there you lunge forward (not on but off of the centerline) and punch.

You see how I cross his line of attack with the 1-2 steps. When I attack I stay off his line of attack and hit at an angle.

1-2-3 & Attack. I add one more cross step and then lunge in and backfist. When you look at the above photos (solo and partner), go from photo 3 to photo 4A to photo 5 and you will see the addition to the sequence.

1-2, Rear foot & Attack - I add the rear foot going to the opposite direction and then come in with a back fist.

1-2-3, Rear foot & Attack - I add the rear foot going to the opposite direction and then come in with a punch

Offensive footwork or entry footwork: straight entry and deceptive entry. I divide entry footwork into 2 parts:

Straight entry is your basic go from here to there with no stops in between kind of footwork. You can either explode and go in full speed or measure the speed of your entry to ensure some kind of safety on your way in. My general rule of thumb is that the closer you are, the faster you take off. The further you are, the more you measure your entry. I show the straight entry footworks in the chapter on Positioning.

Deceptive entry is where you use offensive angle stepping, creeping into range, and broken flow types of footwork. Offensive angles are good for an opponent who is a strong counter attacker along a straight line. I'll demonstrate the angle actions I teach in my school. The first is to angle past your opponent and hit.

Angle Action #6 - Angle past and hit.

Beyond Kick & Punch - The Complete Fighting Principles Of American Freestyle Karate

Angle Action #7 - Step and angle in. Here you step off at an angle and then go straight at him from that angle.

Angle Action #8 - Step and angle past. You take a shallow angle step with your lead foot, angle step across his line of attack and hit.

Angle Action #9 - Zig zag step. You do a staccato series of short angle steps across his line of attack and then hit on the last step.

Angle Action #10 - Step forward and angle past. You slide up with your rear foot and then angle past and hit (to the left [3] or right [4]).

There are all sorts of variations to this. Creep steps (as shown in chapter 3) are good for that opponent who doesn't know range. You cunningly get inside of their firing line and then explode on them.

Broken flow is good against experienced fighters as their reactions are generally pretty fine tuned. You can break the flow by either halting your entry for a split second and then going in on the pause or changing speeds of your attacks, etc. There are many ways to break rhythm. Let's go over the concept of Broken Flow (often referred to as *Broken Rhythm*) at this point as it needs clarification.

rhythm - an ordered, recurrent alternation of strong and weak elements in a flow of sound and silence in speech.
flow - a smooth, uninterrupted movement.

What has been the key element in the difficulty of learning the concept of Broken Rhythm is that it has been a misnomer, an incorrect title for the action you are trying to learn. No one fights in a robotic, rhythmic beat. They will fight in a continuous action, a flow. What has been taught as Broken Rhythm is, in fact, *Broken Flow*. A combination is a flow of action. An entry footwork is a flow of action. Even if it is an explosive action, it is still a continuous action. When you break up this continuity, you have Broken Flow. 4 types of Broken Flow (by no means complete):

Timing break - interruptions in a single technique or a series of techniques within a flow.
Speed break - Speeding up or slowing down within a flow of action.
Motion break - stopping and restarting.
Energy break - breaking up your opponent's flow or composure or not allowing your opponent to set up a flow or composed state of mind.

Beyond Kick & Punch - The Complete Fighting Principles Of American Freestyle Karate

Example of a combination being a continuous flow of motion.

right punch begins...   *...pauses*   *...resumes*

Example of Timing Break - interruptions in a single technique or a series of techniques within a flow.

Example of Motion Break - stopping and restarting.

So, what *is* Broken Rhythm? It is when another *breaks into* or *interrupts your rhythm*. The easiest example of this is first you set up a rhythm *you can feel* by bouncing.

A relaxed bounce needn't be more than an inch or so off the floor. I overemphasize it for photo depiction.

Defensive Broken Rhythm: You have set up your rhythm. If your opponent comes at you without matching your precise rhythm, you will feel it and can respond. It will be as obvious as someone singing a different note than you. You set up a rhythm. Their action breaks into/across your rhythm.

I spotted this while warming up for a tournament match one time. I set up a rhythm and spotted that my partner never matched my rhythm when he came in at me. I either hit him right when he came or stepped out of the way easily. I told a friend of mine who was fighting in the heavyweight division, Mike Shintaku, about this. Mike used this and ended up winning his division by just this tactic alone. We met in the Grand Championship match. The crowd booed us for the apparent non-action. We were waiting for the other to break rhythm.

I set up a rhythmic pulse. He doesn't match my rhythm when he comes in. This actually breaks into or across my rhythm and alerts me to his advance. I draw back and hit him as he comes in.

How to use *rhythmic entry* by matching his rhythm. *Offensive Broken Rhythm #1*. You match the rhythm of your opponent's bouncing. This will create a rapport (def. relation marked by harmony, accord, affinity or conformity). Without changing your rhythm you attack. The mutual-ness of both of your bouncing will hide the take off. You just don't break the rhythm.

He matches my rhythm. His forward movement is at the same time as my up movement and his action is disguised.

Offensive Broken Rhythm #2. You can also do the above without doing a matching rhythm. You time your take off to match his rhythm. He is doing the bouncing and your moment of entry is matched with his bouncing.

Here he is just timing my rhythm. His attack comes right as I begin my up bounce.

To recap, Broken Flow is where you break up your own flow in order to offset your opponent.

Defensive Broken Rhythm is when your opponent breaks into your rhythm which alerts you right away.

Offensive Rhythm or "match rhythm" is where you match your opponent's rhythm and use it to hide your attack.

All of your entries are for the purpose of getting into hitting range of your opponent. If you can use both straight and deceptive entry you will find something that will work on any given opponent.

Defensive Footwork is a forte of mine. I use 4 different kinds: full retreat, measured retreat, limited retreat and defensive angling.

Full retreat is a full speed backwards, get-out-of-there action which I drove everyone in the Northwest crazy with for so many years. Nobody could catch me. Even at my advanced age I don't know of anybody who can catch me when I'm going backwards at full speed. National champions Keith Vitali and Steve "Nasty" Anderson were good at this also.

Full retreat

Measured retreat is where you tailor your speed to keep just out of range of your opponents reach so that you can counter him in between his attacks. I was good at this also. I'd go backwards just out of range and my opponent would get frustrated and leave himself open while attacking and then I'd slip in the point. I won many a match that way.

Example of Measured Retreat. I retreat at the same speed he comes in at, maintaining a safe distance. Then I counter attack.

Limited retreat is to use one or two steps only when I backed off. I'd do this to make my opponent miss by a hair and then counter him.

Limited retreat. I back up just enough to make him miss and then counter him.

Defensive angling is just getting out of your opponents path of entry as they attack. The difference between a footwork set up and a defensive angle is that in the former you move first and in the latter he moves first. Either way you are still repositioning the target. That is the idea. If you assume the viewpoint of "I'm getting out of the way," you are moving because you have to. If you assume the viewpoint of "Well, I'll just move this target over here now," you are doing it because you want to, not because you're being forced to.

Here's a great example of this. In an interview for the first Ali-Frazier fight Joe Frazier was asked if he thought Ali's movement would bother him. Frazier told them it wouldn't because he was going to put a lot of pressure on Ali the whole fight and that Ali would be moving because he was forced to move. Frazier said, *"There's a difference between a fighter who moves because he wants to and when he's moving because he's being forced to. He won't be able to get his timing, his rhythm, because he's moving because he's forced to."* In the 1st fight Frazier beat Ali by forcing Ali to move instead of letting Ali lead the movement.

Muhammed Ali (left) being forced into the ropes by Joe Frazier's pressure.

Get the idea? Do your angling because you want to park your body over here for a change, not because you're going to get hit if you don't. 3-time national champion Keith Vitali was excellent at this. Remember what I said before. You want to have enough room within which to move and you want to angle right when you recognize your opponent's beginning *motion*, not his commitment. Here are the defensive angle actions I teach at my school.

Angle Action 1 - Lead angle step, front punch, rear punch.

Angle Action 2 - Spin off, lead backfist, rear punch (application shown on next page).

Beyond Kick & Punch - The Complete Fighting Principles Of American Freestyle Karate

Angle Action 2 application

Angle Action 3 - Switch step, lead punch, rear punch. Note: The first punch of this angle action is not meant to hit but to distract your opponent as he comes in. The punch is aimed precisely between the eyes. I have found that most people flinch when a punch or fake is aimed right between the eyes so ensure your punch is on trajectory.

Beyond Kick & Punch - The Complete Fighting Principles Of American Freestyle Karate

Angle Action 4 - Lead side step, rear ridge hand strike, rear punch.

Angle Action 5 - Rear side step, lead punch, rear punch.

Offensive/defensive footwork and footwork set-ups are largely mechanical operations instead of broad sweeping concepts but I include them because without a knowledge of them you will easily fall prey to them. Efficient footwork depends on an understanding of footwork and skill in the preceding principles outlined in this work.

The most incindiary series of matches had to be against Jimmy "Gato" Tabares (R) from Texas. This photo is from our second meeting, the 1979 Battle Of Atlanta in Atlanta, Georgia.

7. KNOWLEDGE OF OFFENSIVE AND DEFENSIVE APPROACHES

sub-principle: How to set your opponent up for a technique is senior to the technique itself.

The definitive work on this subject is my book: **American Freestyle Karate: A Guide To Sparring**. I go over approaches again in **Fighting Tactics & Strategies**. You could consider those two books a greatly expanded chapter 7, so to speak. You should get both of these books in order to gain a full conceptual understanding of this subject.

I am, however, going to go over the general concept here. An approach is a method of going about doing something. There can be an approach for doing anything, let alone fighting. Whenever you face off with an opponent, they will use some approach or another to attack you or defend themselves. When you look at fighting using approaches, you don't worry about techniques, just the approach they use.

The offensive approaches are: Direct attack, Attack by combination, Indirect attack, Attack by trapping, and Attack by drawing.

The defensive approaches are: Hit as your opponent changes, Hit as the ranges cross, Hold your position and hit , Simultaneous block and counter, Block and counter, Evade and counter, and Evade. I'll give a definition and illustrate each one. (Note: Attack by combination and Indirect attack will be lengthy as I include the combinations and fakes I teach my students.)

Direct attack – Direct attack is your singular attack, picking out a target and going for it.

Attack by combination – two or more attacks, each intending to land.
Punch combination #1 - Lead punch face, rear punch body, lead punch body, rear punch face.
In the following pages I will detail Punch Combinations 1-10, Kick Combinations 1-10, Hand & Foot Combinations 1-10, 1-2 fakes 1-6, and Faking By Numbers 1-8. I use these in my school to get across the idea that there are many, many different ways you can put the moves you know together. Once you have learned these, they serve as a template for any kinds of maneuvers you wish to create. They are also great coordination training.

punch combination #2

punch combination #3 *punch combination #4* *punch combination #5*

Punch combinations 2-5 - The top row is punch combination #2; back fist, rear punch. Each additional combination adds one more punch to the mix. Punch combination #3 adds another back fist. Punch combination #4 adds a palm hook to that. Punch combination #5 finishes off with a front hand punch to the body.

Punch combination 6 - Rear hand punch to the body, same hand backfist to the face. This is a speed combination rather than a power one. I taught this to a friend of mine back in high school over 30 years ago. He used it successfully in a fight he had gotten into.

Beyond Kick & Punch - The Complete Fighting Principles Of American Freestyle Karate

Punch combination 7 - Rear punch body, rear ridge hand strike head. The key point in this combination is the double hip rotation.

Punch combination 8 - Backfist, rear ridge hand.

Punch combination 9 - three step charging punch.

Punch combination 10 - Backfist, rear punch body, step through and backfist, rear punch body.

Kick combination 1 - Rear leg front kick, same leg round kick

Beyond Kick & Punch - The Complete Fighting Principles Of American Freestyle Karate

Kick combination 2 - Low round kick, same leg high round kick.

Kick combination 3 - Rear leg angle (or round) kick, spinning back kick.

Kick combination 4 - Step up round kick, side kick.

Kick combination 5 - Step up side kick, round kick.

Kick combination 6 - Step up double side kick.

Kick combination 7 - Step up low round kick, high hook kick.

Beyond Kick & Punch - The Complete Fighting Principles Of American Freestyle Karate

Kick combination 8 - Step up high hook kick, high round kick.

Kick combination 9 - Rear leg front kick, hook kick.

Kick combination 10 - Step up side kick, hook kick.

Hand & foot combination 1 - Step up front kick, lead hand punch, rear hand punch, rear leg round kick.

Beyond Kick & Punch - The Complete Fighting Principles Of American Freestyle Karate

Hand & foot combination 2 - Rear leg angle kick, front hand punch, rear hand punch.

Hand & foot combination 3 - Step up round kick, backfist, rear punch.

Beyond Kick & Punch - The Complete Fighting Principles Of American Freestyle Karate

Hand & foot combination 4 - Standing side kick, back fist. This is for when your opponent stands too close to you.

Hand & foot combination 5 - Step backfist, side kick, spinning side kick, rear hand punch.

Beyond Kick & Punch - The Complete Fighting Principles Of American Freestyle Karate

Hand & foot combination 6 - Two step punches, rear leg round kick.

Hand & foot combination 7 - Advance backfist, advance backfist, spinning back kick. I use this when my opponent measures his retreat. I set him up by using a short footwork and then hit him with a longer range technique.

Beyond Kick & Punch - The Complete Fighting Principles Of American Freestyle Karate

Hand & foot combination 8 - Lead step, lead punch, rear punch, rear leg foot sweep, grab and rear punch.

Hand & foot combination 9 - Slide up, knee & elbow guard, set forward and rear punch, step through backfist, rear punch.

Hand & foot combination 10 - Slide up rear punch, rear leg front kick, set forward backfist, rear punch, rear leg side kick.

Indirect attack – using a distraction of any kind to set up your opponent for the follow up attack.

1-2 Fakes #1 - Slide up lead leg front kick fake, lead hand punch.

1-2 Fakes #2 - Rear leg front kick fake, rear hand punch.

Beyond Kick & Punch 1 The Complete Fighting Principles Of American Freestyle Karate

1-2 Fakes #3 - Slide up lead punch fake, rear punch.

1-2 Fakes #4 - Slide up rear punch fake, lead punch.

1-2 Fakes #5 - Slide up lead punch set up, lead leg front kick. This is for an opponent who blocks from too far away.

1-2 Fakes #6 - Lead step rear punch set up, rear leg front kick. This is for an opponent who blocks from too far away.

Beyond Kick & Punch - The Complete Fighting Principles Of American Freestyle Karate

Fakes by numbers 1 - Slide up round kick fake, backfist.

Fakes by numbers 2 - Step up side kick fake, backfist.

Beyond Kick & Punch - The Complete Fighting Principles Of American Freestyle Karate

Fakes by numbers 3 - Spinning back kick fake, backfist, rear punch.

Fakes by numbers 4 - Ridge hand strike fake, angle punch.

Beyond Kick & Punch - The Complete Fighting Principles Of American Freestyle Karate

Fakes by numbers 5 - Rear punch to body fake, head punch.

Fakes by numbers 6 - Scoop kick to the groin fake, high round kick.

Fakes by numbers 7 - Angle (or round) kick fake, front kick.

Fakes by numbers 8 - Step up and wind up hook kick fake, side kick.

Attack by trapping – you use an obstruction or capture of some kind to set up your opponent for the follow up attack.

Attack by drawing – you draw your opponent into attacking prematurely, leaving an opening in their defense and attacking that.

In this example I leave my head open for his strike. Right as he moves I cover his strike and counter with a punch of my own.

In this example I leave my head open again. As he comes forward for his strike, I angle my head to the side and counter punch.

The defensive approaches are:

Hit as your opponent changes – Your opponent makes any kind of a shift whatsoever, you attack. I put this into a defensive category because you are responding to his action rather than setting him up for it. This could be considered a pre-emptive strike.

In this example he raises his hands, getting ready to move. Just as he does so I come in with a side kick.

Hit as the ranges cross – You move forward as he moves forward and hit him at mid distance.

In order to hit me, he has to cover the entire distance I set between us.

I step forward just as he moves and hit him mid distance. This appears dangerous but it isn't. He will time his attack to land when he covers the distance to me. By knowing this, I actually hit him mid his own attack.

Hold your position and hit – Your opponent comes forward and you hold your ground and hit.

Simultaneous block and counter – You block/parry his attack and hit him as the same time.

Block and counter – You block/parry his attack and counter attack in a 1-2 motion.

Evade and counter - You remove the target he is hitting at and counter strike him. This is done by stepping or body shifting. Angle actions 1-5 (demonstrated earlier in this book) are what I teach to my students as templates to this approach.

Evade – You move away from his attack without counter attacking.

Usually fighters tend to use the attacks and defenses that feel the best for them and not do the awkward or the unseemly methods. This locks them into certain and specific ways of doing things. And that "lock" will trap them if they are faced with a fighter who understands approaches.

Example: Your opponent is a great counter fighter. He uses block and hit (defensive approach) with great skill. You see this and instead of you going in there, attempting to blast your way through (attack by combination), and possibly getting nailed by this block and counter, you instead fake and attack (indirect attack). He goes for the fake and you hit him with your follow up attack as he is blocking. You get the idea?

Any type of offense or defense goes under the heading of an approach. Kicks, punches and blocks are techniques. Approaches are senior to techniques. They will tell you the mode or style of attacking or defending that your opponent will use. Most karate, kung fu, and taekwondo people do not know that they are locked into a mode of operation. This makes them easy to read and counter if you can read approaches.

Remember one thing. Approaches go beyond any style of karate, kung fu or taekwondo. It doesn't matter if a person does Japanese, Okinawan, Korean, or American karate. An approach is an approach. A direct attack is a direct attack whether it is a kick coming at you or a double leg takedown. It's an attack coming straight at you.

If you become skilled at recognizing approaches, you will start finding out that usually any fighter will stick to no more than three, maybe four approaches at the most and that's all they will use. This should help you when you compete against a person you don't know. Don't worry about his side kick. Check out how he is going to deliver that side kick. How is he going to get it from him to you? If you can recognize that, then you will be able to handle it with relative ease.

Learn to use and recognize the different offensive and defensive approaches.

Battling my good buddy, Al "Hot Dog" Harvey in the final match for the team championship at the 1974 International Karate Championships in Long Beach, California. I barely won by one point.

8. MECHANICS

sub-principle: You need to know how to move the body in order to move the body well.

This is the eighth and most basic of the principles of American Freestyle Karate. This is what you work on all of the time. Your kicks, punches, stances, blocks and so on are your basics and the point from which you start.

Your first 9 months in training are the most important, I feel. This is where you begin to learn your basics. This is also where you create your own habits, good or bad. I say *you create* your own habits because the teaching of the basics does not vary. You work from White up through Orange belt in that amount of time and how much *you* literally follow the instruction is how *you* are going to create your own habits.

Are you sharp? Are you sloppy? Are you going to get it today or are you going to wait until next class? You see what I mean? You create your own habits. They will be either good or bad and they will add up in your further training. If you have created bad habits, then you will spend a lot of time undoing your mistakes before you can test for Black Belt. If you have developed good habits, the time spent on corrections is minimal.

Your mechanics are your tools by which you apply the principles. If your tools are faulty or substandard, it won't matter how many of the principles you know. You need to have your tools in order to work the principles.

The calm before the storm. Benny "The Jet" Urquidez (R) and I before our match for the lightweight title in Denver, Colorado in 1974. Benny went on to become one of the greatest full contact fighters ever.

Afterword

These are the fundamental principles upon which I base my martial arts teaching, my thinking - my way of doing things. As you can now tell I favor the well-rounded approach. If you have a facility in a great many areas you will not become surprised by any of them. My own viewpoint regarding learning and using these principles is IF I CAN DO IT, ANYBODY CAN. My martial arts beginnings are not the most stellar and it's taken me a long time, a lot of traveling around, and a lot of work to get to where I am now. I've always had one thing going for me and that is DESIRE. I wanted it bad enough to go out and get the knowledge, to push through whatever I needed to attain the skill to be where I am today. You all have the potential to be the best you can be. All you need is the willingness to be that, the commitment to do it. This is not over night skill I'm talking about but something which will need time, energy, and experience to fully develop. I use these as guidelines to go by instead of having none.

You'll notice by now that although you can specialize in any one of these principles and be a step ahead of most fighters, they are pretty interdependent. In the use of one, others will come into play also. Still, one can become good at one or two of these and be pretty sloppy in the others. I've seen marvels of mobility who got trashed because they couldn't monitor. I've seen players who had beautiful left/right balance but couldn't hit the broad side of a barn because they had no timing to speak of and their distancing was shot.

In developing your own skills, you can use the preceding principles as a checklist in how you're doing at any particular time. Is your monitoring on? If so, how's the timing? Distancing? Positioning? Balance? Mobility? From there you can do a fast correction and get back on track in a hurry.

I invite you to take the material in this book and try it for yourself. See how it affects your sparring and fighting abilities. Make it yours. This is the spirit in which I present it to you. Good luck.

1967 - 2002
These photos are from my first and last competitions. I'm on the right side in each. The photo on the left is from 1967 in the juniors division and the one on the right is from the 4th Funakoshi Shotokan World Championships in Las Vegas, Nevada, November 2002.

Appendix

The Value Of Kata Training In The 21st Century

(Note: This essay is a preview of my next book which is on motion application of traditional karate kata. DA)

This is a very interesting concept coming from me as I have been one who has loudly questioned the value of kata training at for many, many years. I have, however, changed my viewpoint regarding the value of kata training. Let's look at a little historical background first to create a context.

In the early 1400's, Shohashi combined the three kingdoms of Okinawa into one kingdom. Some 50 years down the line his son put into force a weapons ban. This was to keep down any possible uprisings. In the 1600's the Shimazu clan from Kyushu, one of the major islands of Japan, conquered Okinawa and another weapons ban was put into place. Any kind of cutting tools were placed under lock and key. When the Okinawans needed them for farming purposes, they were checked out at the beginning of the day and checked back in at days end. During this time, the Okinawan fighting art of *te* (hands) was trained in secrecy. The training was to deal with an oppressor who had a weapon and you didn't. If not done like this before, kata was now a way of training fighting techniques. The kata had various scenario settings that were rough to do on a partner.

During the Meiji era in Japan (~1860's), the caste system was abolished and with it, the samurai class. They were forbidden to carry their swords while Japan worked hard on becoming westernized. The fighting arts, the *jutsu,* were fading out and becoming transformed into arts of discipline and self-realization, the *do* (way or path) arts. *Kenjutsu* (sword art) became *Kendo*. *Jujutsu* became *Judo*. *Karate jutsu* became *Karate do*, and so on. Nothing had changed in the performance of the kata thus far. The emphasis on why you were doing kata was beginning to change.

Keep in mind that the orient has a long tradition of spirituality and the pursuit of spiritual freedom. It is, therefore, not surprising that the shift from kata being a compendium of fighting techniques to a method of spiritual development took place. As a training method in the viewpoint of a *do* (way, path), the focus of kata is on concentration, precision of movement, total command of the body, and a way to achieve *mu shin* (no mind). A western description of mu shin would be "to be in present time." To a westerner who wants results right now, the concept of *do* requires a major viewpoint shift.

The founder of karate in Japan was Gichin Funakoshi. He was chosen as the initial exporter of the Okinawan art of karate not because he was the most skilled but because he was very well educated. He helped usher in the viewpoint of kata training for personal development.

In the 1920's Gichin Funakoshi took up residence in Japan and began the transformation of the Okinawan art of Karate jutsu (China hand technique) to Japanese Karate do (empty hand way). A very key change was in what the techniques of the kata meant. The *apparent actions* of the kata; e.g. the inside forearm block, the rising block, the downward block and so forth became the *intended* actions and functions of the movements. This is a very important point. If the move was a downward block in the kata, you trained it as a downward block in application with a partner. Look at all the different books on Japanese karate published up through the 1970's and you will see in the prearranged sparring techniques being done that way. The head punches are blocked by rising blocks; the front kicks are blocked by downward blocks; the mid level punches are blocked by either inside, outside, or knife hand blocks. This is how they were taught. Were the Japanese taught this way because the Okinawans didn't want them to know the actual intent of the actions in the katas? Did they teach one way and do another? I don't know myself but it has the apparancy of that being the case. Look over the pictures on the following page and you'll see high ranking masters using these motions as blocking actions and others of them applying the same motions differently.

In the photos below you can see the differences in application. Knife hand block is more of a grabbing action (row 1). The rising block is used as a jamming action or a forearm strike (row 2). The downward block is not forearm against shin bone but a scoop and capture (row 3). The inside forearm block is more of a close in guard action than an extended block (row 4)

Hirokazu Kanazawa left photo
Kenzo Iwata right photo

Gogen Yamaguchi far right photo
Hironori Ohtsuka middle photo
Choki Motobu right photo

Tsutomu Ohshima left photo
Chojun Miyagi right photo

Yoshitaka Funakoshi left photo
Choki Motobu middle & right photo

These were aspects of kata training I could not reconcile myself to. I was 14 years old and about 105 lbs when I began training and was the only kid in an adults class. My own body size didn't allow banging my smaller bones against larger bones. Then there was the fact that you stepped *forward* when you blocked. If your opponent was coming to hit you, he was coming forward to you so that he could land his strike. What was the purpose of me going to him to block his hit when he was coming to me anyway? This just didn't make sense. Let's continue with the history.

In 1945 the Allied forces won World War II and Okinawa had, again, another people other than their own ruling them. This time it was the United States. Many servicemen learned karate do in Okinawa shortly after the war and they learned the same applications the Japanese did for the kata. As outlined in the introduction to this book, the sparring techniques in the USA did not match with the techniques shown in the kata. Our teachers were told that if you master the kata, you will master the combat but the free fighting was proving otherwise. Bluntly stated, the kata players were getting waxed by the free fighters. This was the era I grew up in. Kata was all but useless to me.

In the late 1970's, articles about pressure point application of kata (tuite jutsu) were getting published. The first person in the USA I recall going public with the knowledge was Seiyu Oyata. Shortly afterwards, George Dillman was publishing articles on the hidden pressure point applications of the moves within the katas. A block was no longer a block; a punch was no longer a punch. There was more. The hidden applications of the kata were based on acupuncture points and meridians and if you manipulated the points in a particular way and succession, you would get a reaction from the body. To my understanding, there are three types of pressure points: ones that get activated by a touch; ones that get activated by a pressure or rub; and ones that get activated by a strike, often at a particular angle and style of impact. An impact on one point of the arm will cause the knees to buckle. A touch on two points of the wrist will interrupt the flow of energy to the grip and so become weak.

A second point being made was that there were many grappling applications in the kata movements. This action was actually a joint lock and not a block.

I was not yet convinced, though. A sticky point of pressure point application for me lies in its complexity. Mind you, I am *no authority* in its theory or application. I can see how the master well trained and well versed in it can make it work but what about the "rank and file" student or novice black belt? A self defense or combat situation is a hot and fast affair with lots of random elements and pressure point application is very precise. Studies have been done and they reveal that when your heart rate reaches a certain beats per minute, you begin to lose fine motor control. (A great book which contains this research is "On Combat" by Col. Dave Grossman and Loren Christensen, PPCT Research Publications, pg. 30) This translates into complex motions go rapidly to the wayside. In a combat situation your adrenaline will kick in and your heart rate will go up. I feel your ability to be pinpoint precise as to where you strike will be greatly impaired. This is why, I feel, kata may have many of the same moves in them – to go over simplicity of application under different situations. I may change my mind in the future regarding pressure point application but in present time I have a hard time with it. (Side note: a student of mine is also a black belt under Mr. Dillman and he is working hard at converting me.) I like to do what I call *"functional application."* Functional application relies on *motion application* and not pressure point application.

I'll take a side path at this point. In my training under Prof. Presas, I learned 8 empty hand kata called *anyos*. These anyos were quite straightforward as to their applications. One of the points Prof. Presas stressed heavily was the ability to make the translation of any action. Often this meant a translation of a stick action to its empty hand counterpart but it also means translating one *motion* to many different applications of that one motion. This became the key for me in Modern Arnis and karate. I'll explain. Prof. Presas was incredibly well rounded. His weapons artistry included blunt impact weapons as well as bladed ones, short weapons as well as long ones. His empty hand art included the full gamut of weaponless fighting; kicking, punching, deflecting, locking, throwing, grappling, body management, sticking, adhering – the works. He was a *master of motion*. Training with him you began to see "this" could also be "that."

It was my training with Prof. Presas where I went from strictly kick/punch focus to a full application of martial motion. Locking, sticking, redirecting, throwing, as well as weapons work brought me to the point where I began to recognize and utilize motion rather than strictly technique. This is where kata opened up for me. If one takes the kata as a format for motion, many applications reveal themselves.

I now take a look at a blocking (or punching) motion and can see it as:
1. a release
2. an entry into a release
3. a lock
4. an entry into a lock
5. a throw
6. an entry into a throw
7. a choke
8. an entry into a choke
9. a punch
10. a grip (flesh, nerve, hair, cloth, etc.)
11. a block

The key to all this is to work off motion. Let's look at the motion for an inside forearm block.

Let's take a look at examples of *motion application* of what appears to be a "blocking action." His right hand grabs your right wrist. You:
1. twist it up and out for a release
2. twist it up to your right, palm punch the arm for the release
3. twist it up, secure his hand with your other hand and center lock
4. twist it up, grab with the other hand and step under for a side by side lock
5. twist it up as you step forward with your left leg behind his right leg, "cross face" him with his grip hand and throw him
6. twist it up and grab his wrist with your right hand and go into a cartwheel throw
7. twist it up, grab his hair with your left hand, pull his head down into the crook of your right arm for a guillotine choke
8. twist it up and hit him, step behind him for a rear naked choke with your left arm
9. twist it up for a release and punch
10. twist it up for a release and grip the side of his neck
11. twist it up and duck behind it for a block (cover)

The above is a template for any kind of motion found in a kata.

Inside block as a release. I roll my knuckles at the end of the move to execute the release.

Inside block as a set up for a release. I go to position and then use a palm punch to effect the release.

Inside block as a (lock) center lock.

Inside block as a set up for a lock (side by side lock).

Beyond Kick & Punch - The Complete Fighting Principles Of American Freestyle Karate

Inside block as a throw. I step behind him and buckle his knee while I run his arm in front of him for the takedown.

Inside block as a set up for a throw (cartwheel throw).

Beyond Kick & Punch - The Complete Fighting Principles Of American Freestyle Karate

Inside block as a choke (guillotine choke)

Inside block as a set up for a choke (rear naked choke).

Inside block as a strike

Inside block as a grip.

Inside block as a block (cover action).

Whether one does a kata from a framework of *do* or *jutsu*, it is a valid method of training based on the viewpoint you wish to pursue it from. Even a western approach of doing kata for stress relief, exercise, intellectual curiosity, or even just for the fun of it is valid. The key is to actually have a reason to do it instead of robotically following instructions just for the sake of form. It's all a matter of viewpoint. For me, the concepts of kata being a grappling application of self defense and applications of the functions of motion now place it back into relevance in modern day self defense training. Free fighting takes care of the squared off, at a distance application of karate techniques, the "fist fight" as you will. Understanding the actions contained in the kata can train you in what to do when someone has a grip on you. Being a free fighter myself, this is quite a shift in viewpoint but that's the wonderful thing about viewpoints – they can shift.

Kata now makes sense when you take in the historical elements and the fact that fighting takes places at all ranges and not just dueling distance. So, if any of you are of a sporting mind, retake a look at any one of your kata and see where any one move can be shifted into something else and I think you'll find that you are on the road to discovering the "secrets" of the masters.

OKINAWAN KATA

In *Martial Arts Training In Japan – A Guide For Westerners,* author David Jones states: *"Japanese karatedo has come to incorporate philosophies important to the Japanese. Whereas modern Japanese karatedoka may philosophize about Zen, "no mind," and satori (enlightenment), the Okinawan stylist, for the most part, was simply trying to hit and kick as hard as possible and incorporated philosophical underpinnings such as ki (intrinsic energy) and hara (the emotional, spiritual and physical center of the body) to assist the primary objective."*

I find the statement about Okinawan karate stylist interesting. At first glance it sounds like a degrade of Okinawan karate as compared to Japanese karate. When you look at historically and culturally it makes sense, though. Again and again I make the point of Okinawa being a farming community as opposed to Japanese culture which had, among its other values, the seeking of perfection through exact ritual. The Japanese tea ceremony is a perfect example. It is not about brewing the perfect tasting cup of tea. Okinawa needed to be pragmatic about training hence the above statement by Mr. Jones.

I favor the Okinawan kata for motion application breakdown. I prefer the classical Japanese and Okinawan kata over the Korean poomse (forms) or Chinese forms. I like the crispness and attitude they are done with. You'll find that a good Japanese or Okinawan kata, performed correctly, can be *felt* by an observer. I use that as a criteria when I observe a kata being done. Can I feel the intention? Do I dare walk in front of the person while he is doing it? If not, they are doing, really doing the kata. Teruo Chinen (Goju-ryu), Akio Minakami (Shito-ryu), and Jerry Gould (Shorin-ryu) are three individuals who exemplify what I am talking about. When they do a kata, the air vibrates!

On a personal note I love the construct of Okinawan Goju-ryu kata. The blend of the power aspects (*go* = hard) and the smooth/firm aspects (*ju* = gentle) within the same kata creates an aesthetic that is hard to describe. Teruo Chinen performing a kata exemplifies this perfectly.

This is the only magazine photo of me doing a kata. This is probably circa 1975.

Also available by Dan Anderson

FIGHTING TACTICS & STRATEGIES: A Successful Champion's Winning Moves, The American Freestyle Karate Way $25.00 & $5.50 shiping and handling.

After 20 years in the making, volume 2 of the best selling book "American Freestyle Karate: A Guide to Sparring", is now printed in hard copy form. This is the long awaited follow up to the longest selling book on sparring ever, American Freestyle Karate: A Guide To Sparing. This new book has been hailed as "The master instructor's text" on the subject and for those of you who like to have something solid in your hands while you read, here it is!

Professor Dan Anderson, a 7th Degree Black belt and founder of American Freestyle Karate has included 20 years worth of technical viewpoints, conceptual aids and other information as well as over 50 sparring techniques. Using over 650, each technique is highly detailed, including original photos taken from actual fights where these techniques were performed.

Here are several emails from people who have bought a hard copy of this book:

Mr. Anderson,
Just thought I'd drop a line to let you know I am really enjoying your book and have improved in some problem areas due to some things I picked up from the book. I have been wanting to key on improving my lead backfist, and blitzing techniques. Specifically the part in your book about the knee-buckle has been very helpful in improving the speed and explosiveness of my blitzing combinations. I had not seen that explanation on the take-off before, and it has really made a noticeable difference. Thanks. Hope everything is going well out west.
best regards, Mark Rudd

Dan,
I received the book. Excellent. I find your explanations of techniques very readable and user-friendly. You provide enough detail so non-experts, such as myself, can really comprehend what you are explaining. Over my many years (although I think you have about 3-4 more years than me) I have seen instructors using some of these techniques, but I guess they were 'secret' because the exact 'how-to', step-by-step was not explained. I appreciate your sharing this knowledge.

Jim L.

I read your second book sparring book. It was awesome. Thanks for your help (directly or indirectly) on my sparring.
John Dickey

DE-FANGING THE SNAKE: A Guide to Modern Arnis Disarms *$25.00 & $5.50 shiping and handling.*

From the author of the bestselling book *"American Freestyle Karate: A Guide to Sparring"*, comes the first Modern Arnis book written by an American. Dan Anderson, a 6th Degree Senior Master in Modern Arnis, has compiled and broken down over 80 disarms including single stick, espada y daga (sword and dagger), reversals and empty hand, into detailed instruction using over 800 Full Color photos. Also included is a history of Modern Arnis and its founder Remy Presas. This book is filled with instructions for anyone with and without experience in Filipino martial Arts and is truly regarded as "The book of basics."

A review by Loren W. Christensen -

There is a proliferation of martial arts books on the market today, some quite excellent and some, well, not so good. The elements that make a martial arts book excellent are clarity of writing, quality of the photographs, and information that fills a need.

As a veteran martial artist of 30 plus years, and a former Top Ten tournament champion, Dan Anderson knows what makes for a good book. He first showed this in American Freestyle Karate, which after 20 years is still the definitive book on sparring, and he shows it again in his newest release, Defanging the Snake: A Guide to Modern Arnis Disarms.

Until now, books on arnis disarming have been few in number and of poor quality. The very thing that readers desperately need - picture quality -- has been consistently lacking.

Now, with the aid of digital photography, the skill of an excellent photographer and masterfully posed subjects, *De-fanging The Snake* brings you perfect images, hundreds of them, so that you can see clearly and exactly what you need to be doing with your feet, body, arms, hands and stick as you execute the perfect disarm.

I've always had a personal philosophy that if I can get just one, usable technique from a book or a seminar, my money has been well spent. Dan Anderson gives you dozens and dozens of techniques in this information-crammed text.

As an author of two dozen books, 13 of them on the martial arts, I highly recommend *De-fanging The Snake: A Guide to Modern Arnis Disarms*.

Loren W. Christensen
LWC BOOKS
www.lwcbooks.com

Letters from buyers of De-Fanging The Snake: A Guide To Modern Arnis Disarms

When I read your books I can hear the Professor's Voice... Thank You
Sincerely,
Chris Rams

Greetings Mr. Anderson,

I recently purchased your Modern Arnis Disarms book, "*Defanging the Snake*".I have been impressed with your presentation of the material in a clear and consise manner. Finally, a martial arts book that delivers worthwhile material in a meaningful way. Thank you for taking the time and focusing your energy so that your teacher will live on for many generations yet to come in part due to your efforts. I am looking forward to your upcoming works.

Peace be with you,
Mark Harrell

ADVANCED MODERN ARNIS: A Road to Mastery *$25.00 & $5.50 shiping and handling.*

Now available in hardcopy format this book is 211 pages with over 1300 bright black & white photos. It comes perfect bound for easier use in training situations and for longer life. When you read the comments below by purchasers of the ebook version, you'll see that this text is the one to have.

"These principles and concepts have been taught to me by Prof. Presas in my over 20 year association with him and are now compiled for all Modern Arnis students as well as Filipino martial artists everywhere to study."
- Dan Anderson

* 8 August 2003 Update *
I just got off the phone with Prof. Wally Jay, Grand Master and Founder of Small Circle Jujitsu. He read the copy of this book I'd sent him, liked it and told me, "You have absorbed your teacher's art." This is high praise indeed as he was one of the "Big Three" (George Dillman and Remy Presas being the other two) and he was a close friend of Remy Presas for over 15 years. The amount of interchange between the two changed both of their arts for the better. Prof. Jay also told me that my description of the three Small Circle Jujitsu exercizes in the chapter on "Two Way Action" were correct as well. I highly value these endorsements and wanted to pass them on to you.
- Dan Anderson

Letters from buyers of Advanced Modern Arnis - A Road To Mastery

The long and short of it, it is clear to me that you are one of the select few who grasped the real genius of Professor's art, that ethereal flow.
- Brett Salafia

The pictures are clear and easy to follow. I have been to many of the IMAF camps, but nobody has a text. that is this easy follow. with all of the photos you can see a great amount of detail.
- Dugan Hoffmann

As with the defanging the snake book this one is really well done. Well presented material and a logical progression from concept to concept, an excellent project.
All the best, John
- John Hoey

I am currently a 1st Dan with Master Chai TaeKwonDo. One of our 3rd Dan's is now instructing in Modern Arnis. I am looking forward to the training added to my 2nd Dan training as well. Thanks. It's a great book!
- Jeff Hentz

MANO Y MANO: The Weaponless Fighting Applications of Modern Arnis *$25.00 & $5.50 shiping and handling.*

Mano y Mano: The Weaponless Fighting Applications Of Modern Arnis: This is the first book ever to be written on the translations of Modern Arnis stick actions to the empty hand. No other book has addressed only the empty hand. With over 1,200 photos and 130 pages, this book covers such topics as: basic offensive and defensive moves and their stick origins, empty hand drills, throwing, empty hand disarming as well as all 8 empty hand forms (anyos) and their breakdown applications.

I would like to thank the following for their contributions of personal forwards: Master Bram Frank, Datu Shishir Inocalla, Senior Master Roland Dantes, Datu Dieter Knuettel, Dr. Randi Schea, Dr. Jerome Barber, Guro Tim Kashino, Guro Rich Parsons and Sensei Jaye Spiro. These are personal contributions and do not reperesent organizational endorsements. Below are brief exerpts from each.

Yours, Dan Anderson

Master Bram Frank - This book fills in the gaps of his other books on Modern Arnis and the martial arts! If you ever wondered how Modern Arnis or Filipino Arts translates into empty hand, well this is the book for you.

Datu Shishir Inocalla - There are not too many authors of Filipino Martial arts empty hand techniques. I am glad that a Master Instructor and a martial arts champion such as Master Dan Anderson has taken this step to write "Mano y Mano - The Weaponless Fighting Applications Modern Arnis".

Datu Dieter Kuettel - In this book he will introduce you into the fascinating world of empty hand techniques of Modern Arnis. Read it carefully and you will pick up valuable information for your training that will enhance your style in the study of Modern Arnis, other Arnis/Kali/Eskrima styles, or even if you´re totally new to the FMA.

Senior Master Roland Dantes - CONGRATULATIONS!
This new book of yours will be another tribute to the legacy of the Philippine Martial Arts. More Power to You!

Dr. Randi Schea - Master Dan Anderson has undertaken the formidable task of trying to efficiently distill some of the key fighting principles that Professor shared with all of us in Mano Y Mano. Dan has organized the principles in a systematic manner similar to his previous books, yet without having to resort to rigid and inflexible doctrines that would be completely contradictory to Professor's Art and his teaching style.

Dr. Jerome Barber - This book on Mano y Mano or the Empty Hand Art of Modern Arnis, is long overdue.

Guro Rich Parsons - Dan's previous books in Karate and Modern Arnis have done an excellent job of doing this and there should be no less expectation with this one.

Sensei Jaye Spiro - In Mano Y Mano as in his other books, Professor Anderson uses an informal, conversational style. The reader is included in his investigation of Arnis empty hand techniques. Professor Anderson thoroughly examines these striking, blocking, checking systems, and sharing his discoveries and analysis with the reader. Anderson comes across as an enthusiastic, down to earth coach, whose goal is to share it all with the reader.

Guro Tim Kashino - This book is a welcome addition to my training library, as are the previous two. Books like these are few and far between. I believe that the Professor would have been very proud of Dan's efforts in the art.

Trankada: The Ties That Bind - The Joint Locking Techniques & Tapi-Tapi Of Modern Arnis

$25.00 & $5.50 shiping and handling.

This is the fourth book in the "Modern Arnis encyclopedia" series and is the first book ever to be written solely on the locking and binding techniques of Modern Arnis. No other book has addressed the last major development of Grand Master Remy Presas prior to his passing, the Tapi-Tapi. With over 180 pages and 1,400 photos, this book covers such topics as: empty hand joint locking, locking with the cane, locking with the legs, pinning your opponent, Small Circle Ju Jitsu exercises, defenses from grabbing and striking attacks, counters to joint locks, the template of the Tapi-Tapi techniques as well as countering the Tapi-Tapi.

Letters from book buyers:

I just received my copy of Trankada: The Ties That Bind. I took it home, put in in my laptop and plunged into it. I had no doubt that this book would live up to the expectations I had. Dan's previous volumes on Modern Arnis were great, and this one was no different. Firstly, I have to say this: Dan, the Professor should have had you writing these books a long time ago. As I have said in the past, Dan's presentation of Modern Arnis is as close to the original as I have seen.

The empty hand locking portion of the book was, in my opinion, the Modern Arnis equivalent to the Chin-na books by Dr. Ming. It was all really well done.

I really enjoyed the tapi-tapi portion of the book. Mostly because it broke tapi-tapi down without my having to get caught up in the "play-slow mo-rewind-play-slow mo" cycle. Everyone should appreciate that, to say the least. I like the how Dan broke it down into reference points and built from there (wish I'd thought of that).

This book, as well as the previous volumes are no doubt THE encyclopedia of the Professor's art. Most important: Dan's books cost about $25. You get at least $100 worth of info out of them. That alone makes them worth buying. I have to say that I anxiously await the companion DVD series. Bring 'em on, Dan!!!

Great book, Professor Anderson!!! Keep 'em coming.

Respectfully,
Guro Tim Kashino

Having just recieved and read my new copy of Trankada, the Ties That Bind, I must echo Tim Kashino's previous comments. This book is well written, and very inclusive. Senior Master Anderson has published a collection of very effective joint locking techniques that include everything from solo practice motions up to applications in Tapi - Tapi, as well as reversals and counters, and all sorts of stick trapping and locking techniques. This book is an all weekend seminar on paper.

The pictures are fantastic, and show the progression of the technique, allowing the reader to understand the flow of the motion. Wherever necessary, Senior Master Anderson has included directional arrows to further assist the reader in deciphering the more subtle points.

Some of this stuff is brutal. After referencing the potential for serious damage earlier in the book, it becomes quite clear that many of the techniques illustrated have the capability to be 'finishers' if properly executed. This is not a children's book.

Dan, thank you for putting this together. This book is a valuable addition to my library, and will be a constant reference for me in my training.

Dan Bowman
Saskatchewan, Canada.

MODERN ARNIS: The Art Within Your Art - The Book Of Basics *$25.00 & $5.50 shiping and handling.*

MODERN ARNIS: The Art Within Your Art - The Book Of Basics is the fifth book in the "Modern Arnis encyclopedia" series and is the most comprehensive book ever to be written on the fundamentals of Modern Arnis. No other book has detailed the origins of Modern Arnis as developed by Grand Master Remy Presas. With over 200 pages and 1,100 photos, this book covers such topics as: striking, basic defense, stances & body shifting, flow exercises, cane anyos (forms) 1-4, classical arnis styles, and much, much more.

Prof. Anderson teaches the "MA-80 System of Modern Arnis" or "Modern Arnis 80." "Modern Arnis, as I learned it from Prof. Presas, stressed several elements, the two most important being the concepts of "The Flow" and to "Counter The Counter." All I have done is taken his art, discerned the fundamental principles which underlie it and put them into a systemized form that will eventually lead the student to developing his or her own flow. This is the legacy my teacher, Remy A. Presas, passed on to me and so I pass it on to my own students."

Book Review

I have known Professor Anderson for almost 4 years now and have been training with him off and on for the same amount of time. From day one, his insight into the art of Modern Arnis has always impressed me; it's almost like being around Professor Presas himself. I had the pleasure of helping him with his first couple books on the subject and was excited when I received a copy of his new one in the mail the other day. What can I say... WOW!!!

The first four books Dan has produced have been top notch and get better by the volume. The Art Within Your Art continues this flow and is by far the best of the bunch. Even though Anderson calls this The Book of Basics, the way the information is presented though words and images makes me feel like I'm reading a book for grandmasters.

There are so many cool things about this book I would love to share, but I will only share one; you will have to buy the book to get the others. One of the things that make this book special is Appendix B. Professor Anderson has included a copy of 15 pages from his own handwritten notes taken when he was training with Professor Presas. You will not find that in any other martial arts book.

I suggest adding this book to your library, no matter what level of training you are at. There is something for everyone.

Mish Handwerker
Chief Instructor
Handwerker Ryukyu Kempo
Vancouver, Washington USA

Available of tne CSSD/SC Website

The Bolo Volumes One and Two
In this DVD series, Master at Arms Bram Frank will introduce you to the bolo. The bolo is a tool used by the Bolo Battalion in the Philippines. You will learn some basic history of the bolo in this DVD series as well as techniques that will translate to Modern Arnis training with the stick. In this DVD, Bram Frank has chosen to give his view of the bolo as it relates directly to Modern Arnis as taught by Professor Remy Presas. Professor Presas often referred to Bram as the man with the knife. As a student of Modern Arnis on any level, this series will introduce you to the blade art and make you appreciate Modern Arnis even more. *$49.00*

The Gunting - An Instructor's View
In this 3 volume trilogy, Master At Arms Bram Frank gets up close with the Gunting. By close up shots and detailed explanation, he will show the instructor and the end user how to best use this unique tool. Using Andy Wires and Peter Roman as examples, Bram shows exactly why the Gunting is quickly becoming a favorite among the military, LEO's, correction officers and other organizations around the World. Each video is approx. 50 minutes in length. 3 videos plus Spyderco Presents for a total of 4 videos *$99 plus shipping*. Each DVD is approx. 50 minutes in length.

Gunting by Bram Frank
Bram Frank along with Spyderco have collaborated to create the GUNTING - The first knife to be designed for self defense. In this three videotape series you will learn the ins and out of the basics of what Sal Glesser, President of Spyderco call a watershed event for knives. Each video is approx. 50 minutes in length.
3 videos plus Spyderco Presents for a total of 4 videos *$99 plus shipping*

Conceptual Knife: The Modular System - DVD
In this DVD series, you will be introduced to Bram Frank's new modular teaching system using his new fixed blade knife the Abaniko. In <u>volume one</u> you will learn flow drill, flow drill in reverse grip, six count, edge out and 12 count. In <u>volume two</u> you will learn three count, reverse grip, backwards, mirror image and backwards - backwards. In <u>volume three</u> you will learn highline drill, hubud, basic disarms, stirring and 5,6,7. In <u>volume four</u> you will learn blocks, 2-3-12, slash and cover, slash and cover drills and passing . In <u>volume five</u> you will learn 5-2-4, backwards 5-2-4, unequal, variations, 5-6-7 & 5-7-6. In <u>volume six</u> you will learn passing & flow drill, countering a disarm, backwards stirring, 1-2-2 backwards and the use of two knives. This series will help you to understand and teach mankind's oldest friend. These DVDs are broken up into chapters, so you may skip to each section for review. *$149.00*

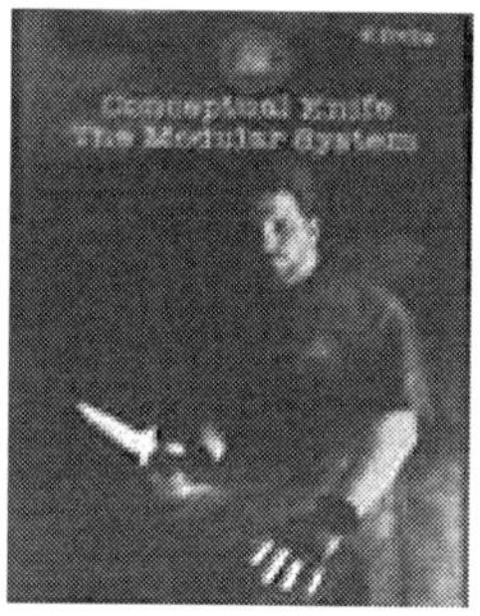

Common Sense Self Defense/Street Combat presents The Conceptual Series
The conceptual series is a set of 5 tapes that Bram Frank did several years ago that cover the conceptual part of training. These are a great addition to your video collection.
<u>Tactical Knife Volume 1</u> (1 hour 10 minutes) & <u>Volume 2</u> (50 minutes) covers techniques of the tactical folding knife. These videos show flow drills, knife self defense techniques, and proper use of the folding knife. 
<u>Conceptual Stick</u> (1 hour) Bram teaches you the basics of Arnis in this video. He covers the 12 basic striking points as well as disarms.
<u>Conceptual Knife</u> (1 hour) This video focuses in on the fixed blade knife. Bram really shows his knowledge inn this training video.
<u>Conceptual Empty Hands</u> (45 minutes) Bram Frank teaches you his theory on empty hands. He goes over the techniques of "open" and "closed". All 5 videos only *$99 plus shipping*

Made in the USA
Lexington, KY
03 November 2013